GUITAR TUNES MADE EASY
by William Bay
MB22096
BIG NOTE/ LARGE PRINT EDITION

Visit us on the Web at www.melbay.com or billsmusicshelf.com

2 # Table of Contents

Numbers = Frets

3rd String
Open

2nd String
1st Fret

1st String
Open

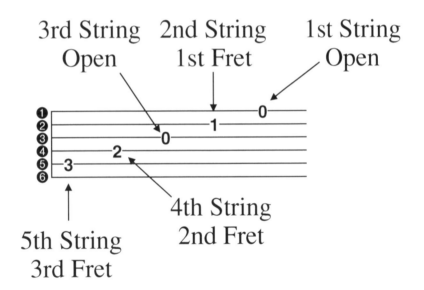

5th String
3rd Fret

4th String
2nd Fret

Notes + TAB

Notes + Time
Values →

TAB →

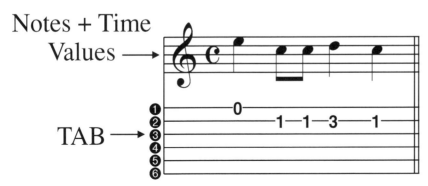

4

Chords Used

C

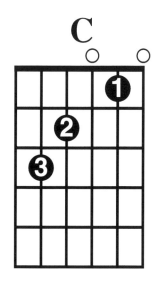

F

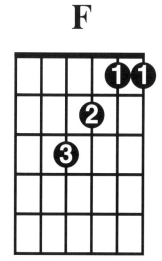

G

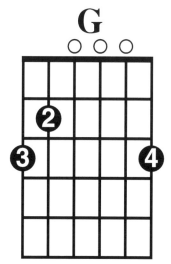

D

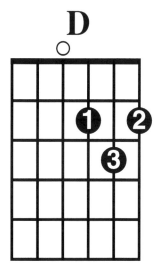

A

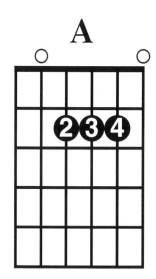

E

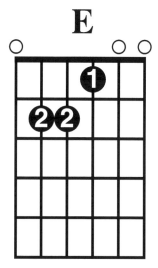

B♭

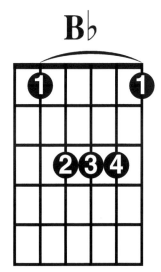

Chords Used

Am
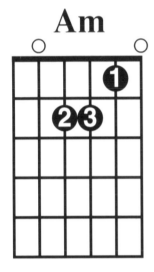

Em
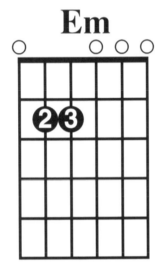

Dm
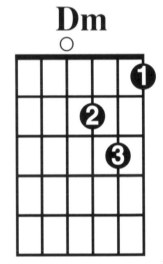

Bm
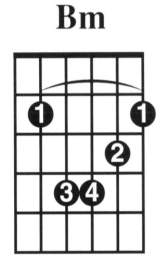

G7
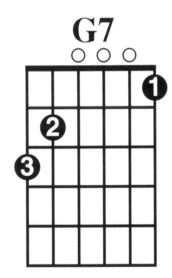

A7
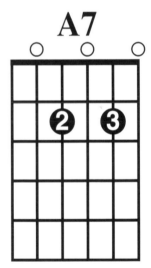

D7
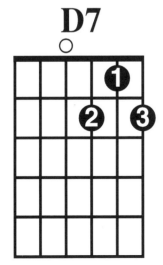

Chords Used

E7
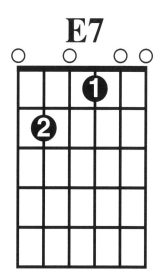

F♯7
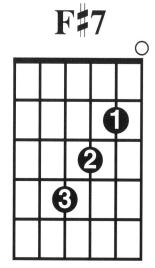

C7
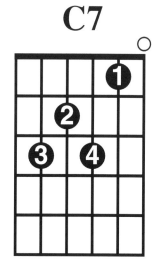

B7
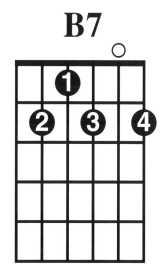

E7sus
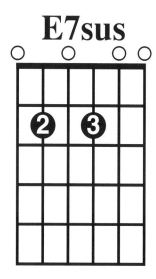

Daug
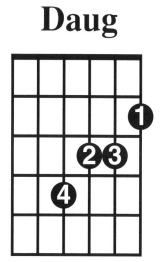

F♯°
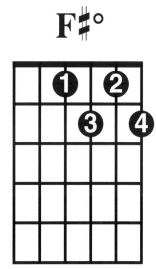

G°
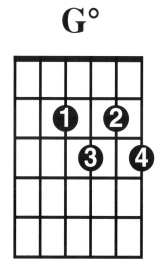

Lonesome Valley

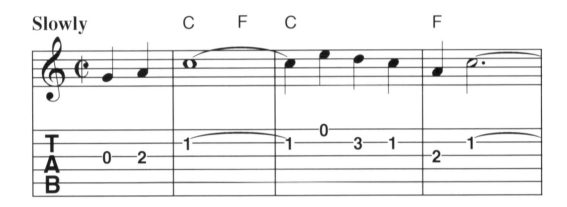

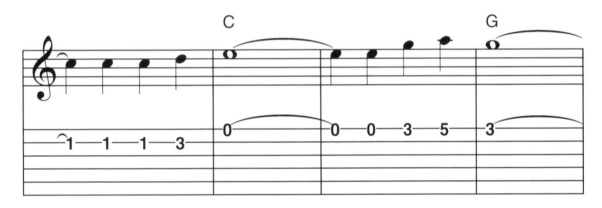

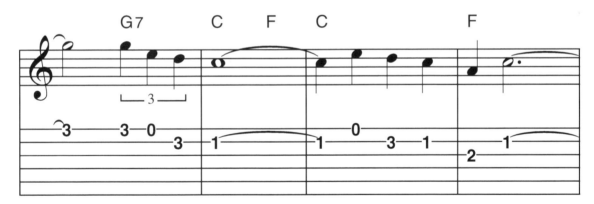

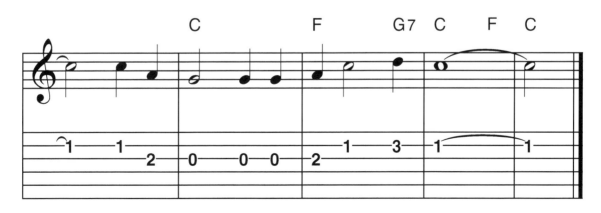

The Sally Gardens

8

Santa Lucia

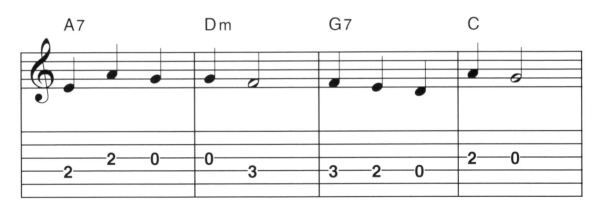

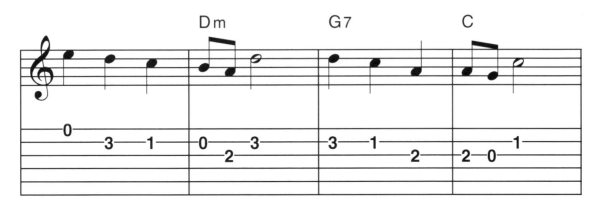

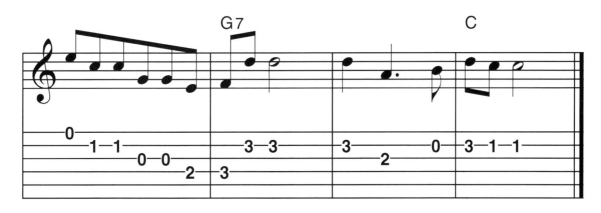

10 Hold To God's Unchanging Hand

Johnny Has Gone for a Soldier

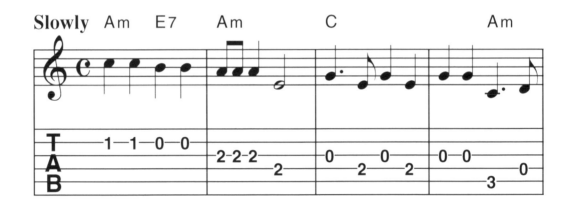

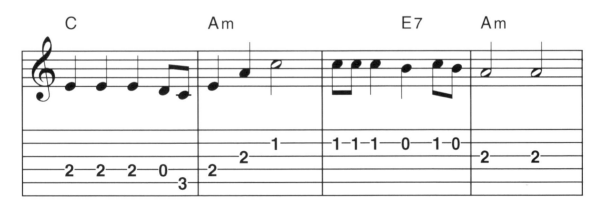

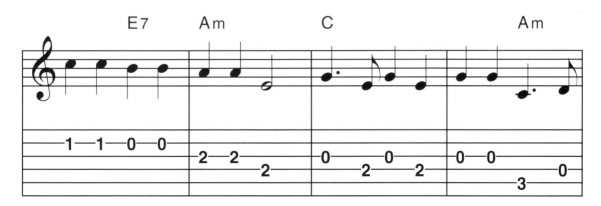

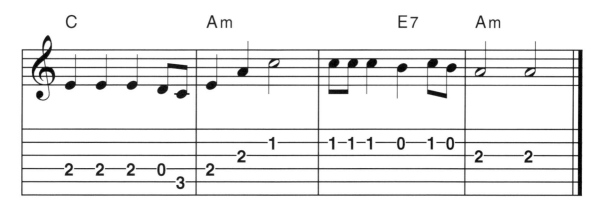

I Am Bound for the Promised Land

Moderately

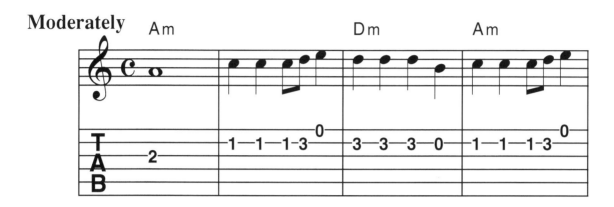

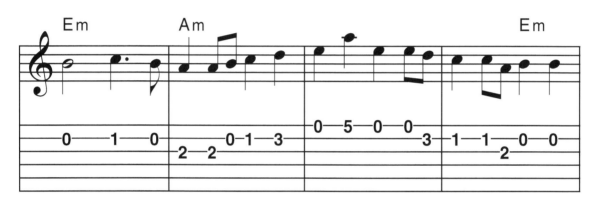

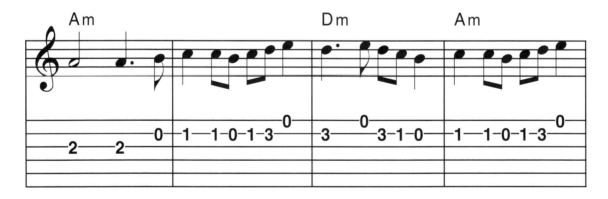

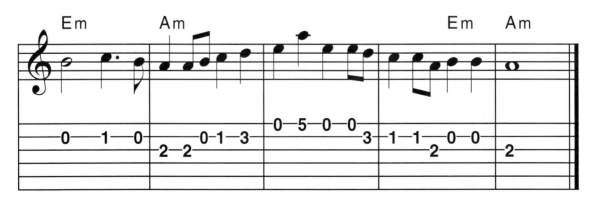

Hatikvoh

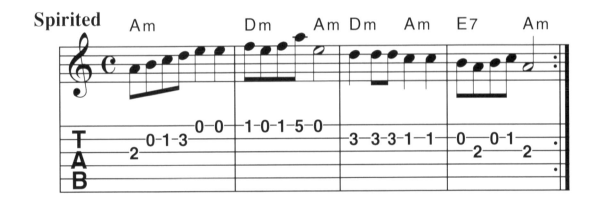

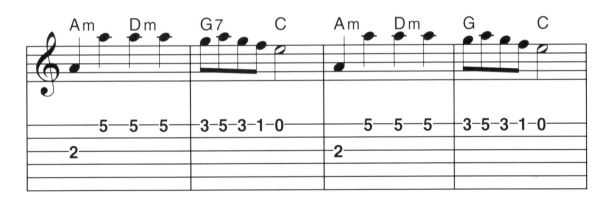

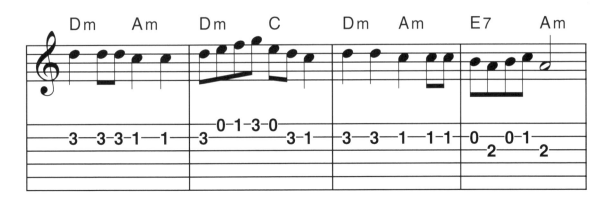

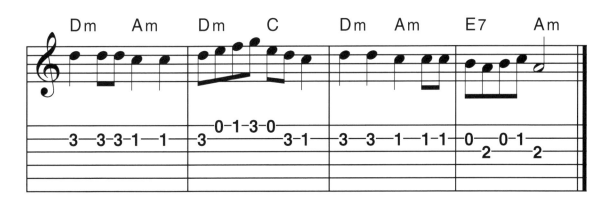

14 Sourwood Mountain

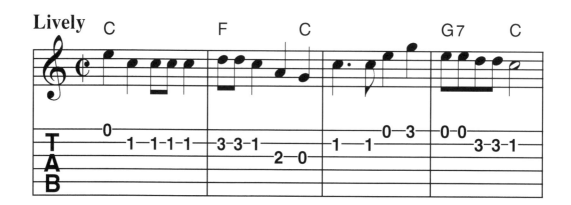

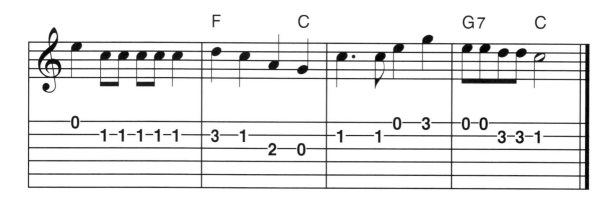

The Fish of the Sea

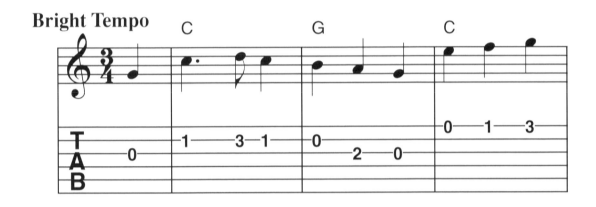

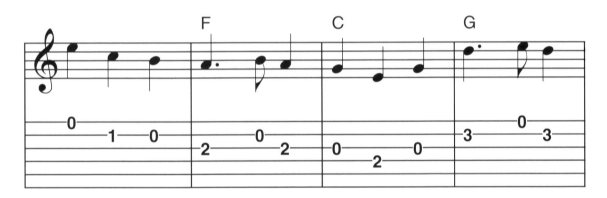

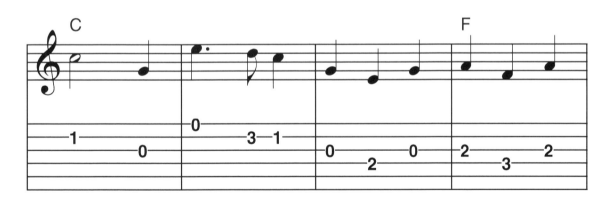

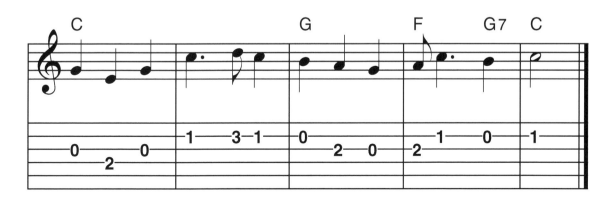

America

Majestically

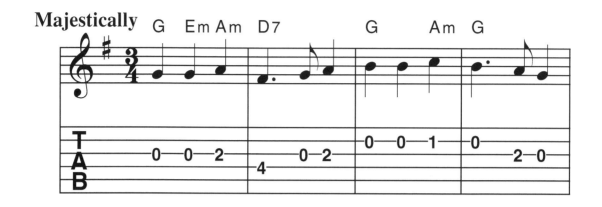

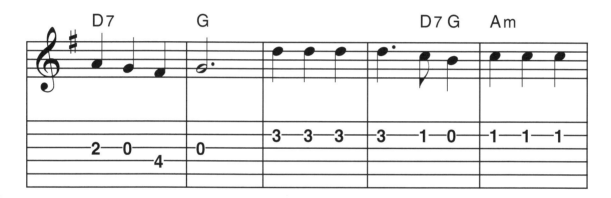

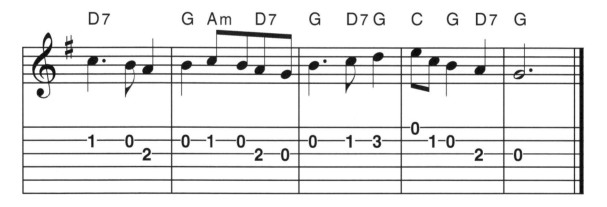

Eyes of Texas

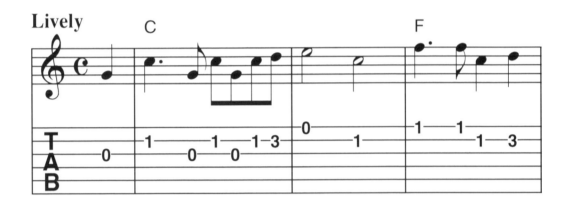

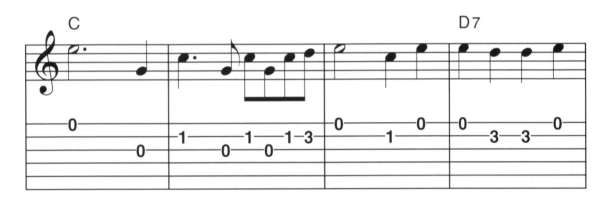

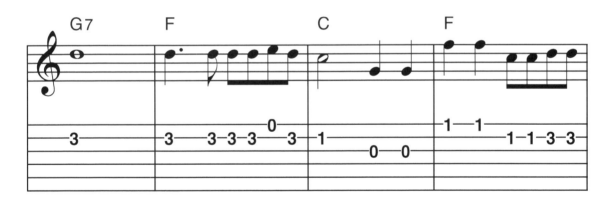

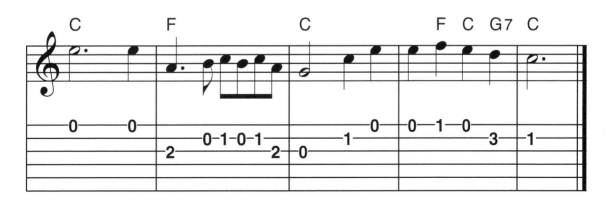

Railroad Bill

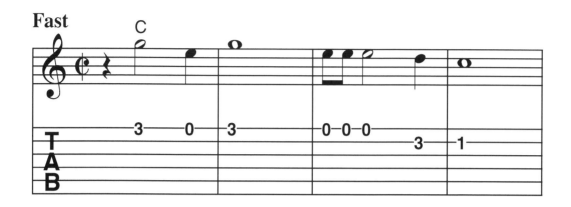

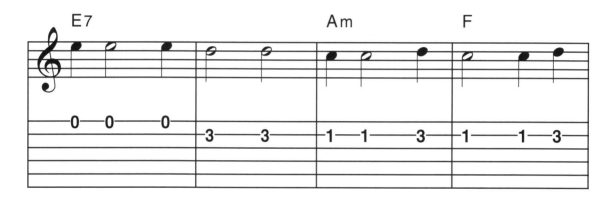

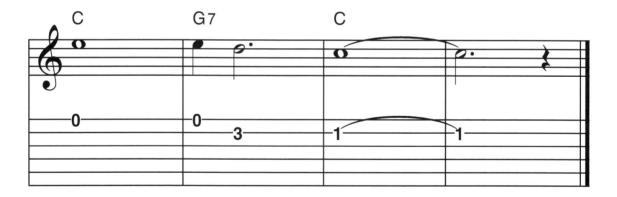

Rock of Ages

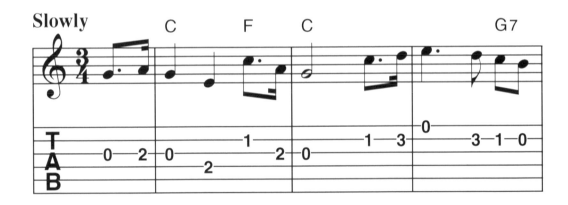

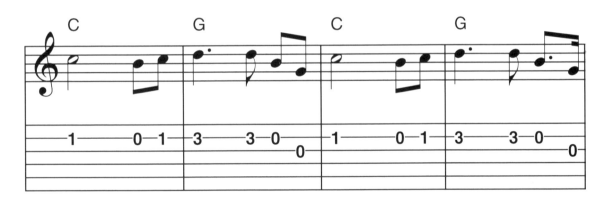

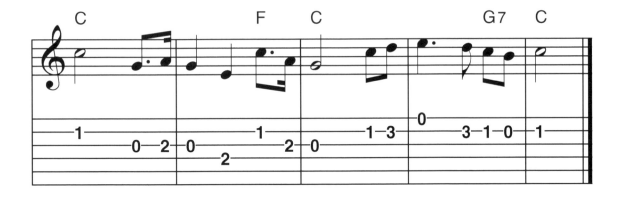

20

America the Beautiful

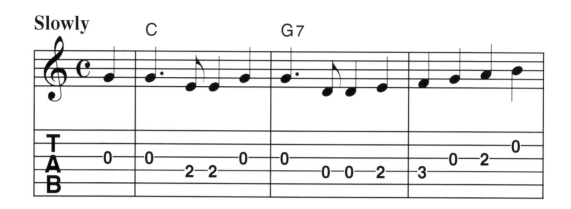

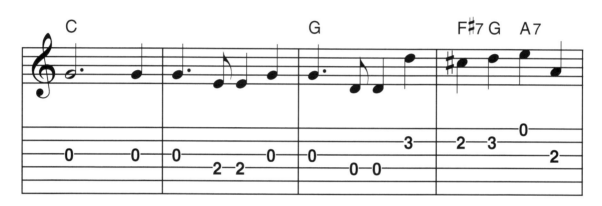

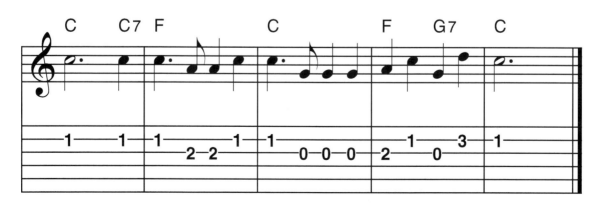

Give Me Oil in My Lamp

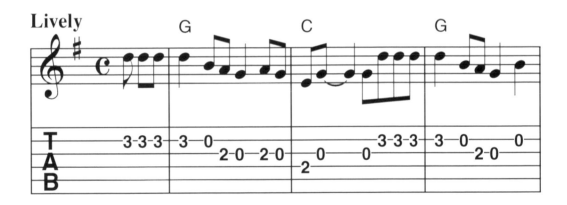

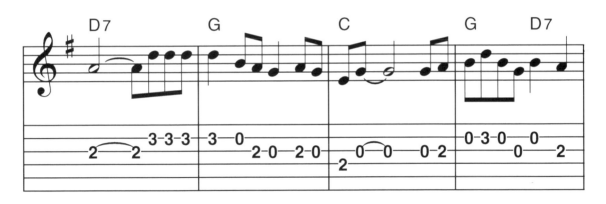

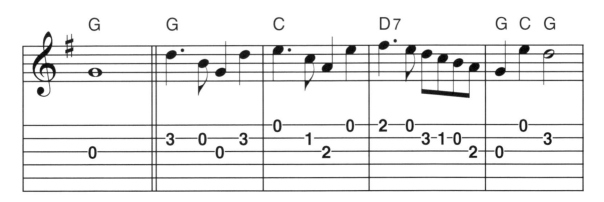

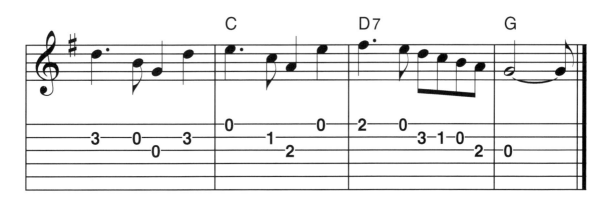

22 Goin' Down the Road Feeling Bad

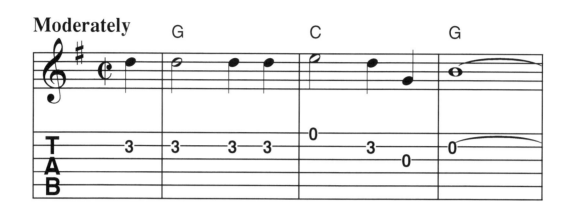

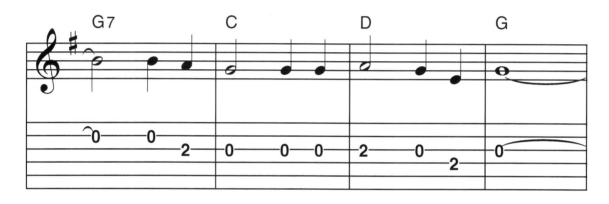

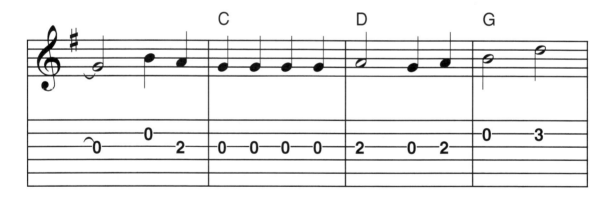

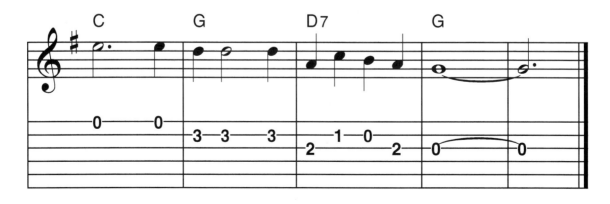

Swanee River

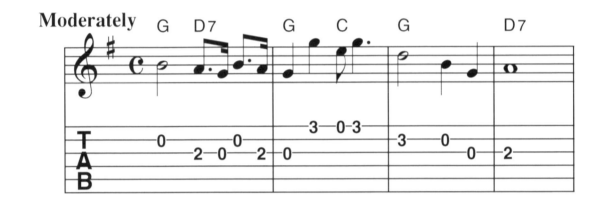

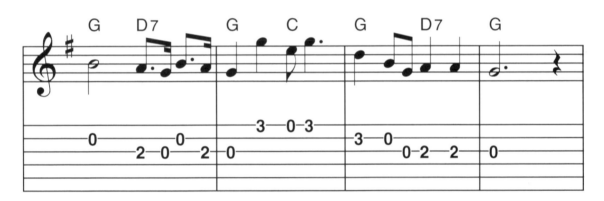

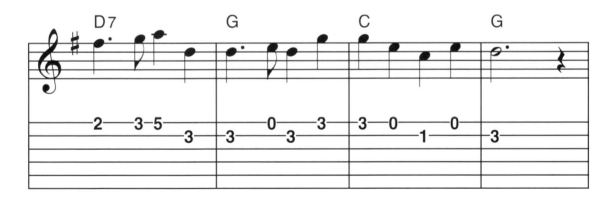

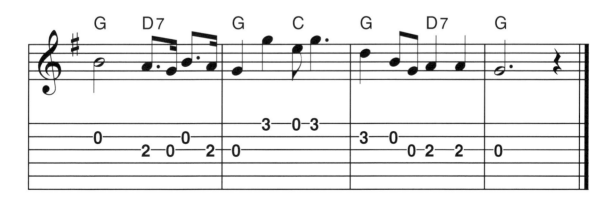

24

My Home's Across the Smoky Mountains

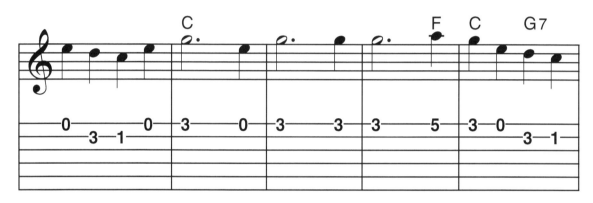

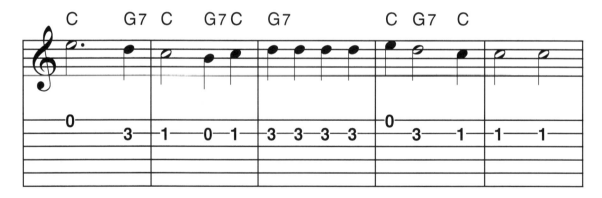

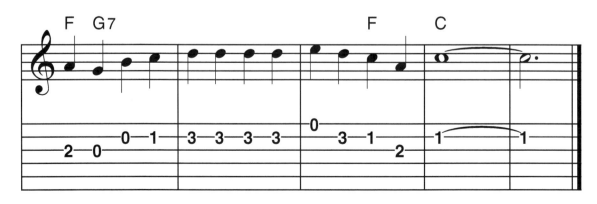

Rise & Shine

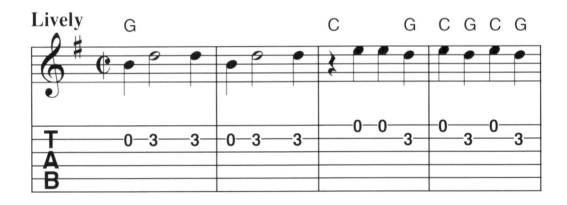

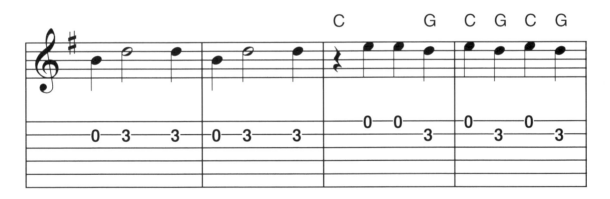

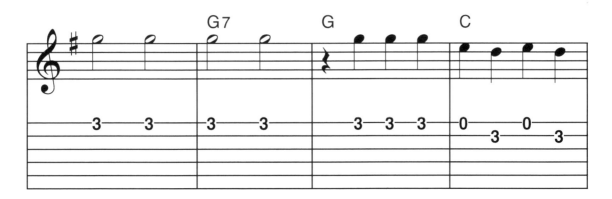

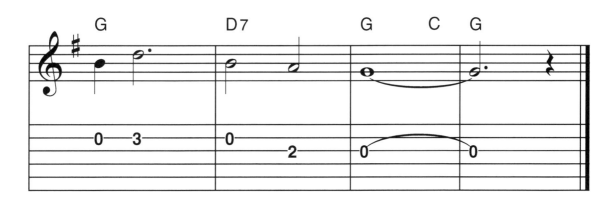

26 This Little Light of Mine

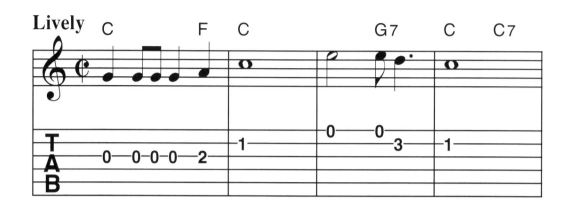

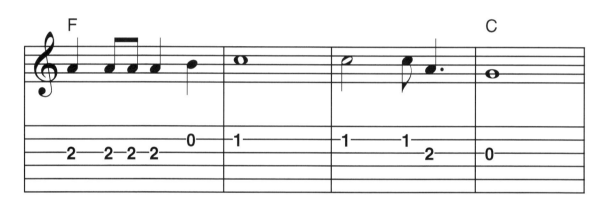

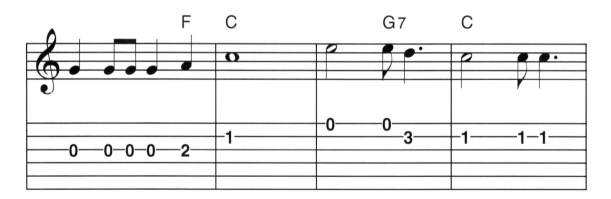

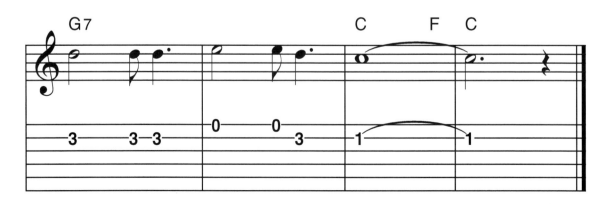

Yellow Rose of Texas

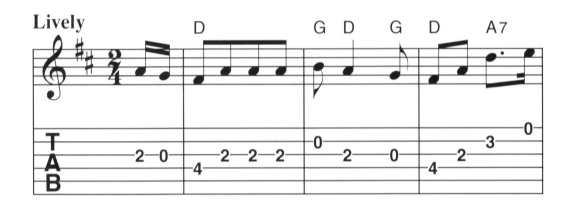

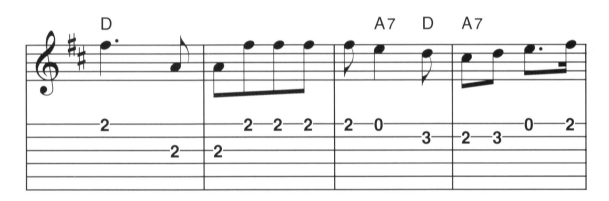

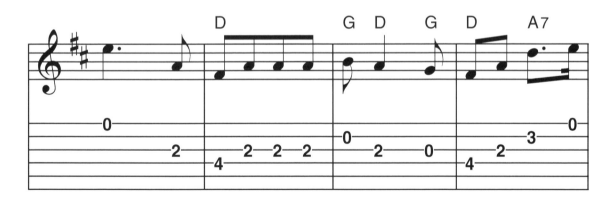

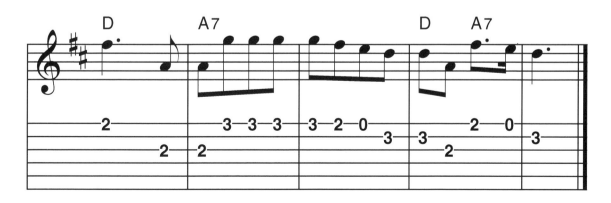

In the Garden

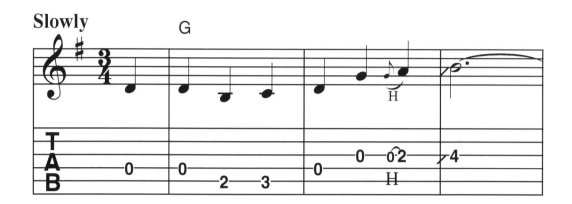

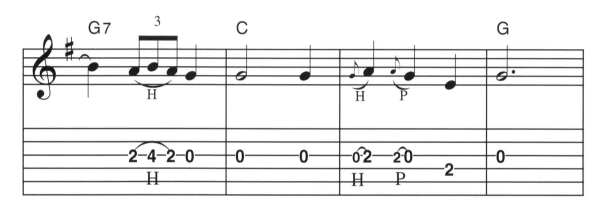

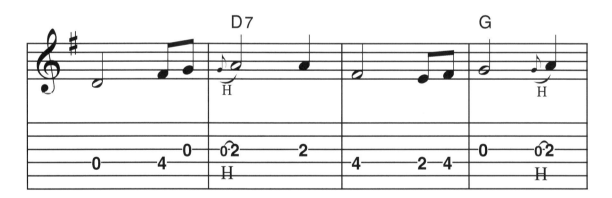

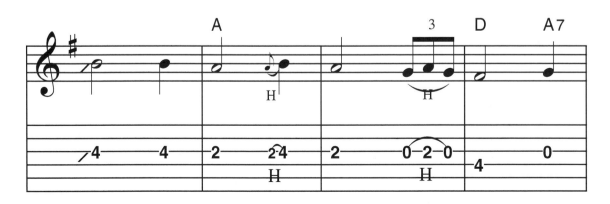

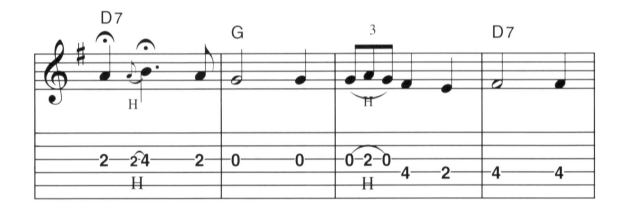

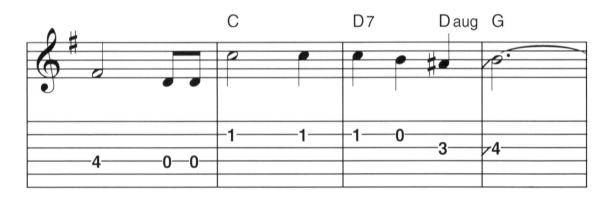

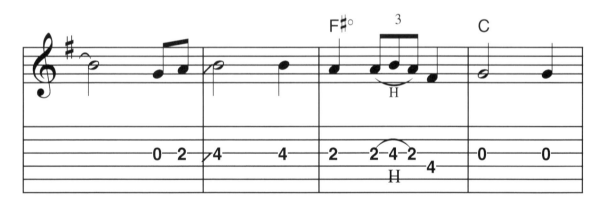

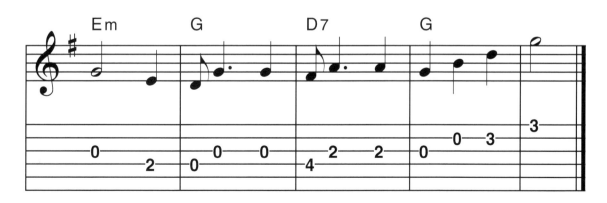

30 # Sweet Betsy from Pike

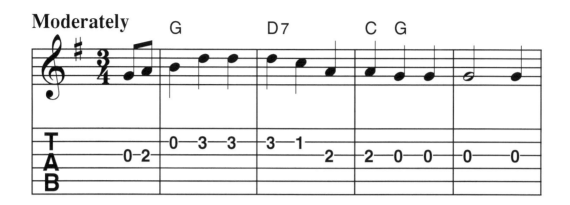

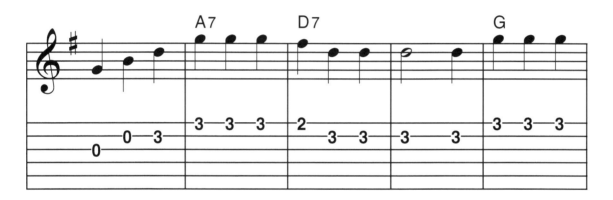

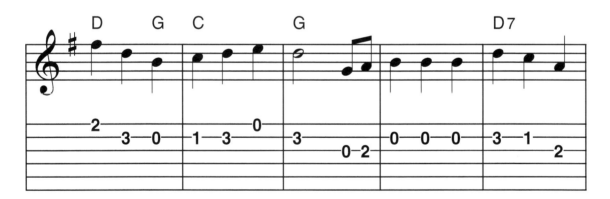

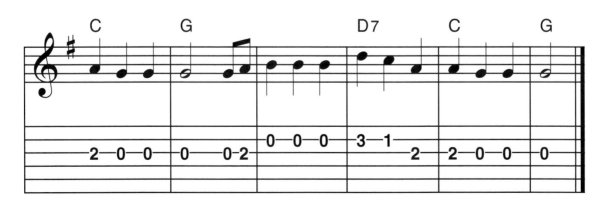

Far Above Cayuga's Waters

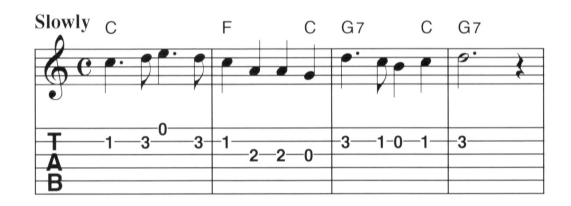

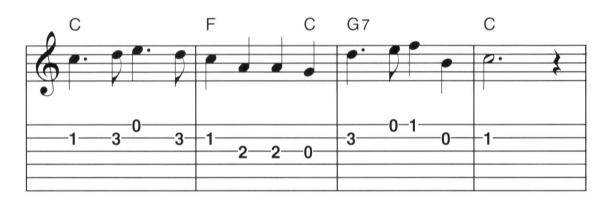

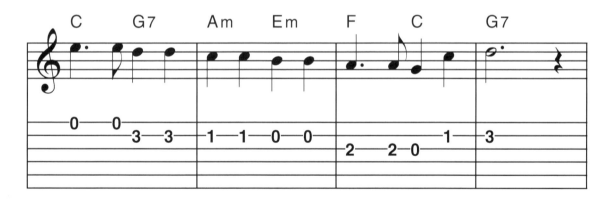

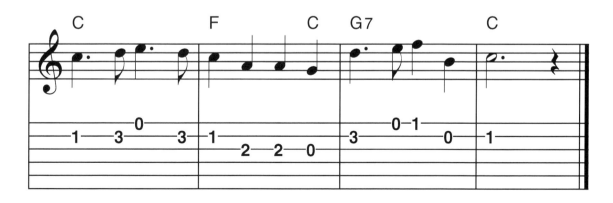

32 She Wore a Yellow Ribbon

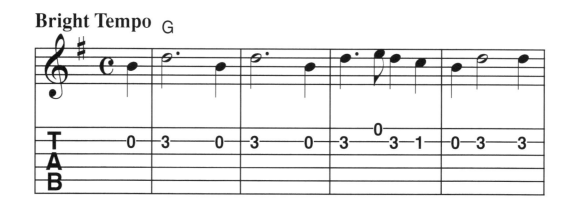

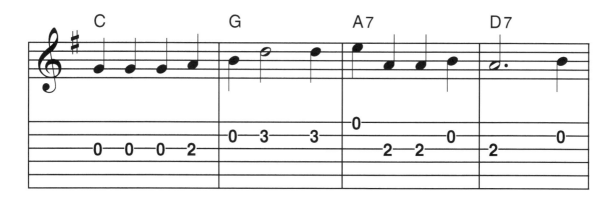

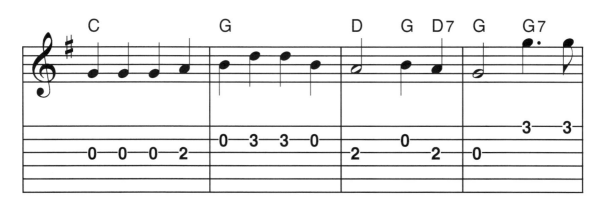

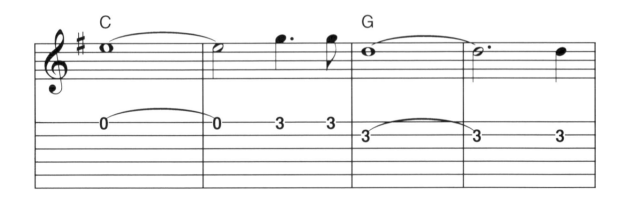

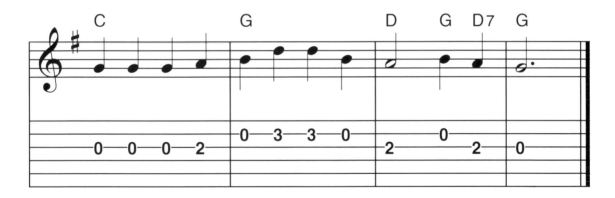

34 She'll Be Comin' Round the Mountain

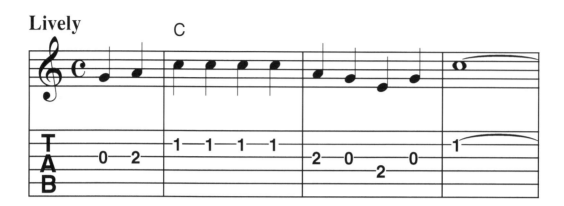

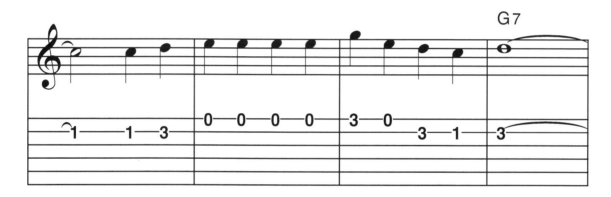

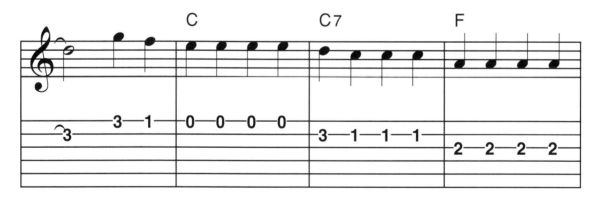

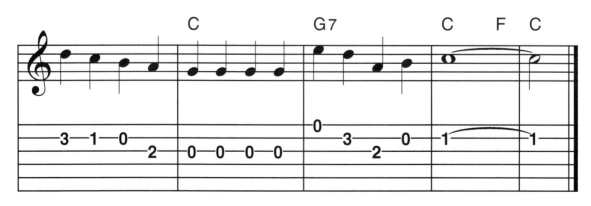

I Feel Like Traveling On

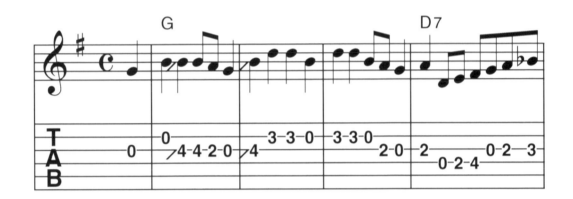

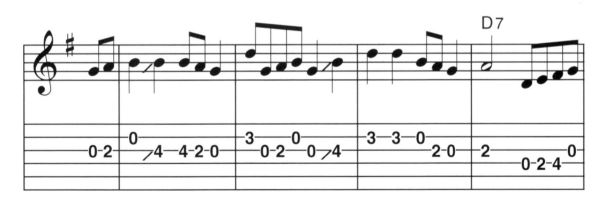

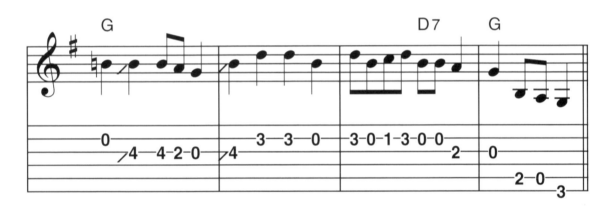

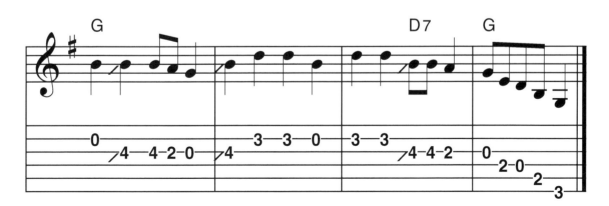

Red River Valley

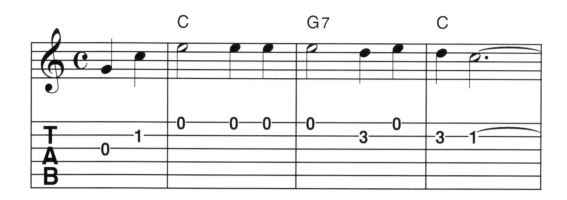

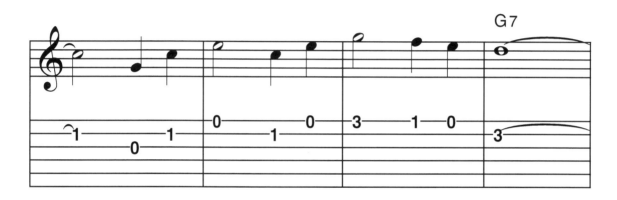

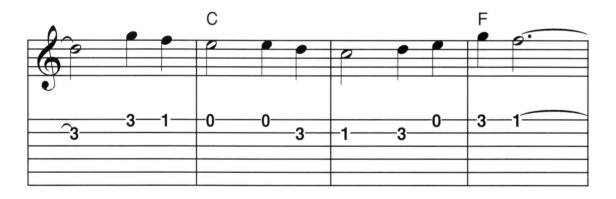

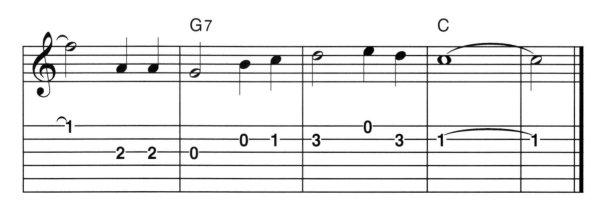

On Top of Old Smoky

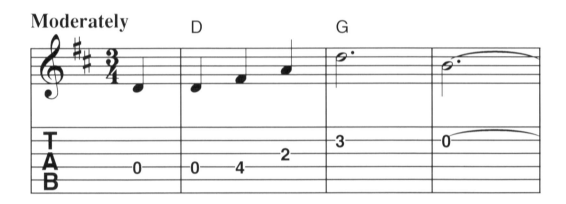

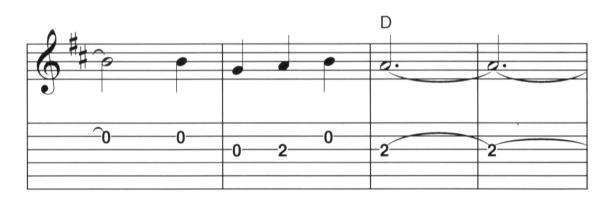

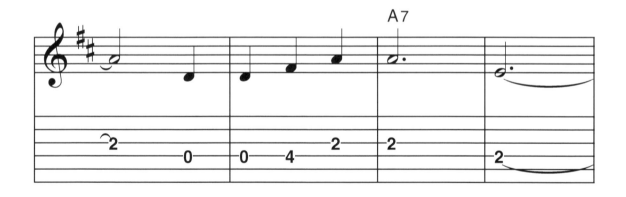

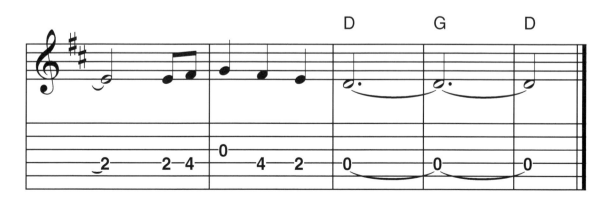

Home on the Range

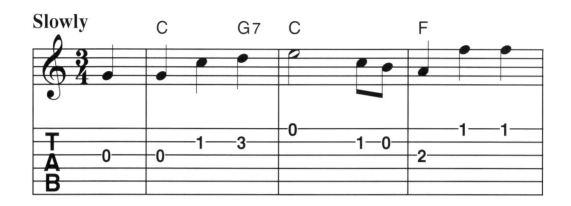

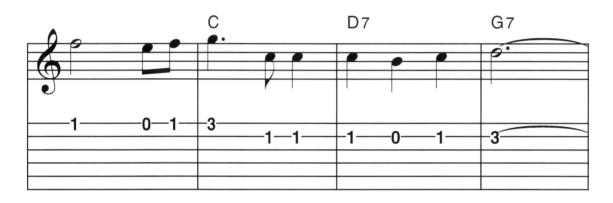

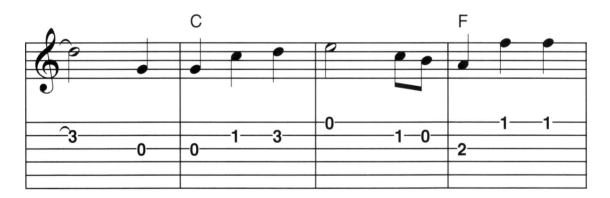

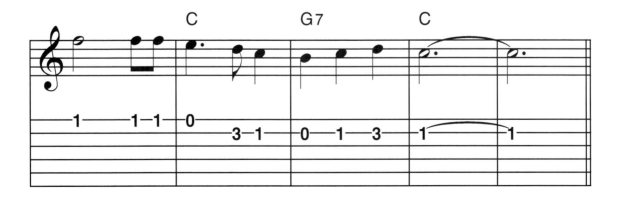

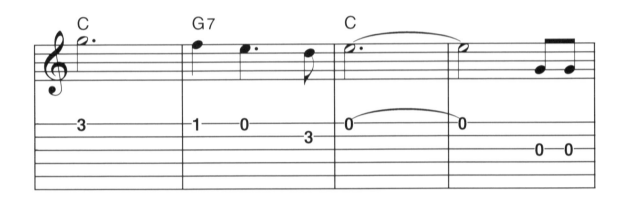

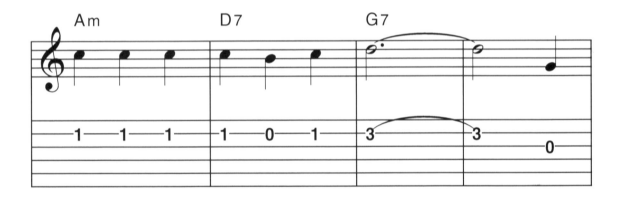

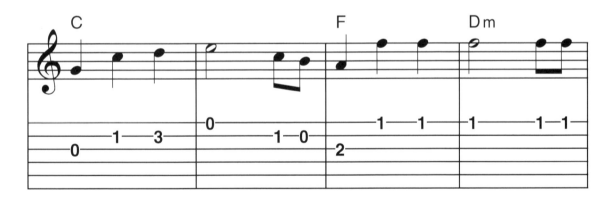

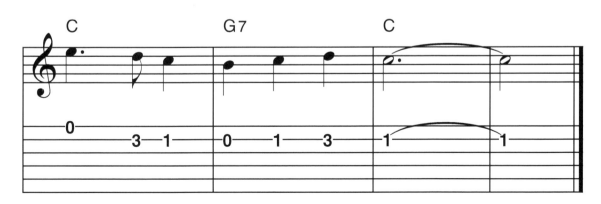

Amazing Grace

Moderately

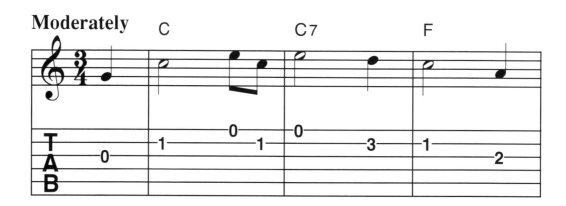

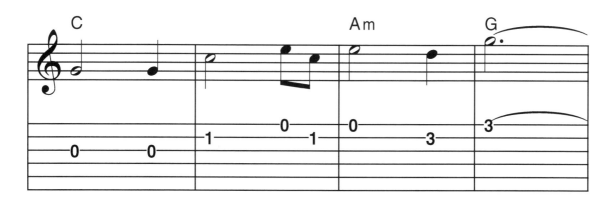

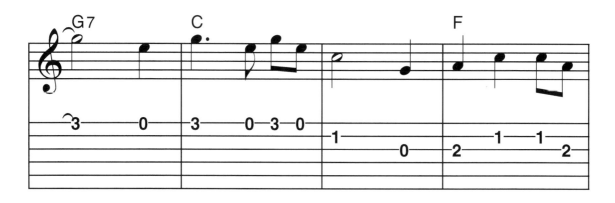

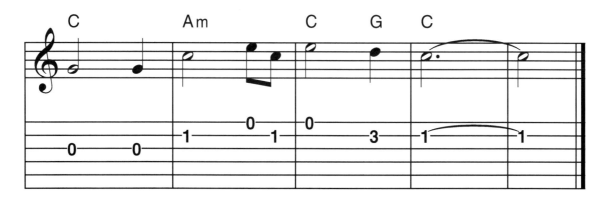

Swing Low, Sweet Chariot

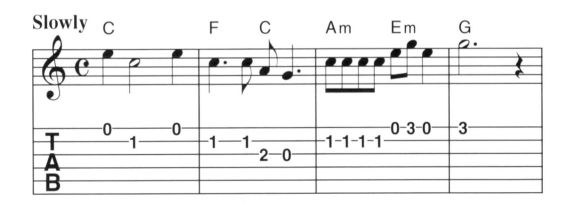

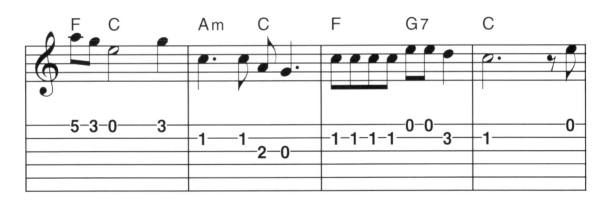

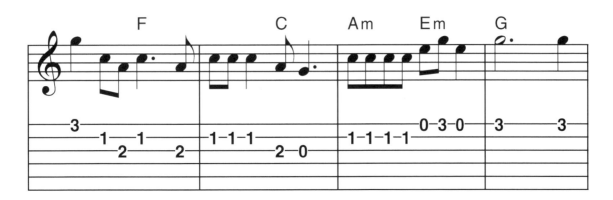

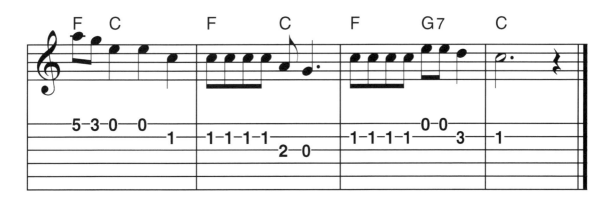

Swallowtail Jig

Bright Tempo

Come & Go with Me
to that Land

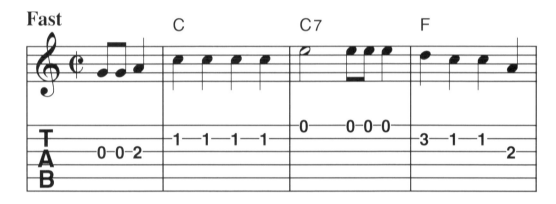

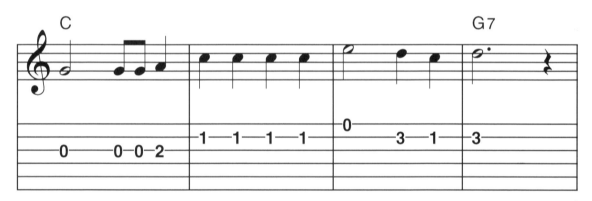

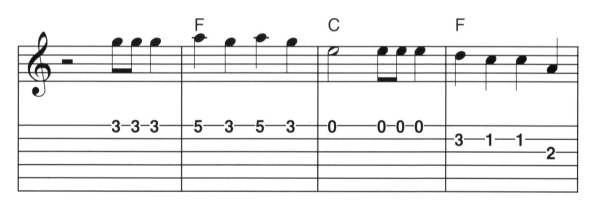

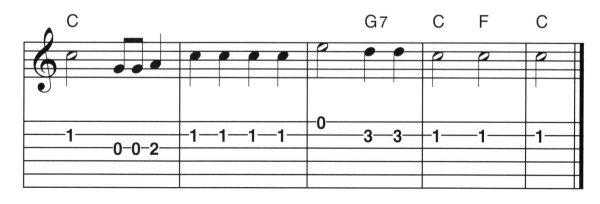

44 Bile 'Dem Cabbage Down

Moderately

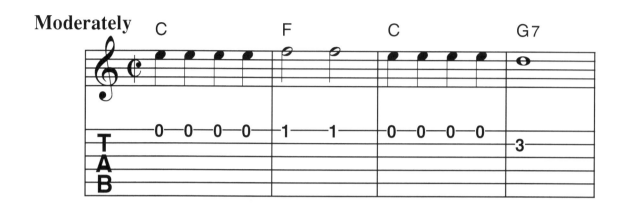

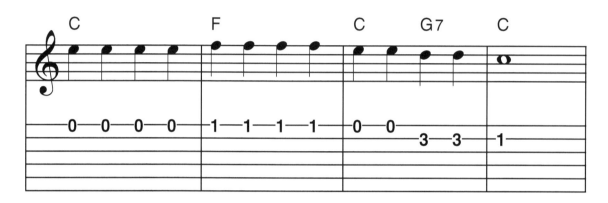

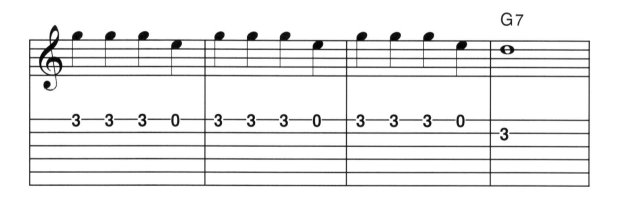

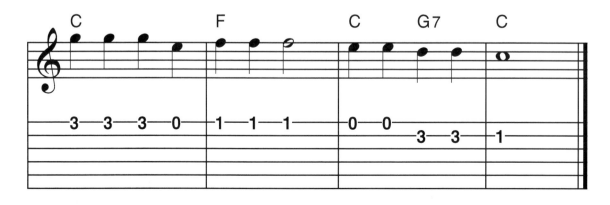

The Unclouded Day

46 # Beautiful Dreamer

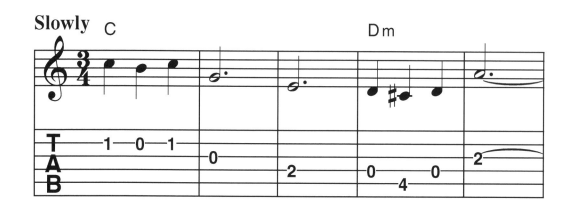

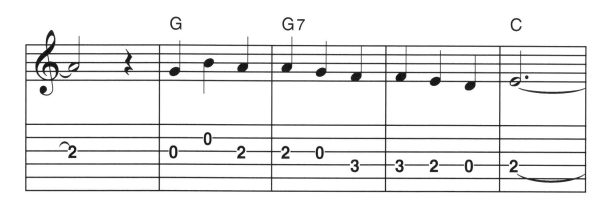

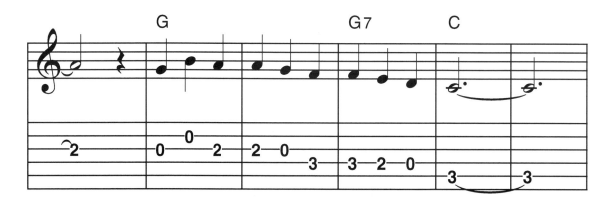

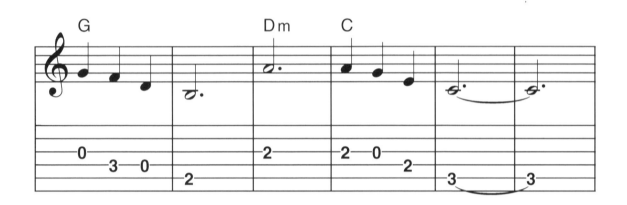

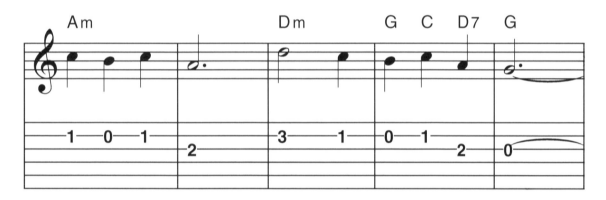

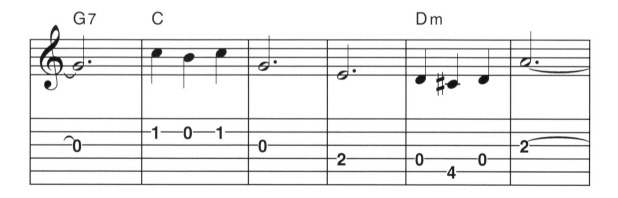

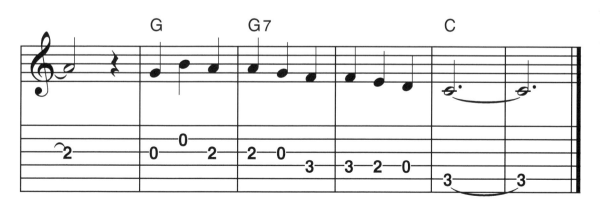

48

Auld Lang Syne

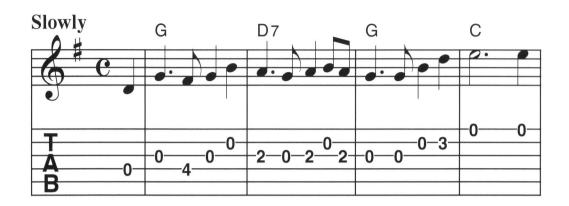

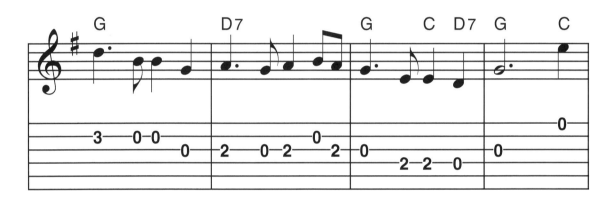

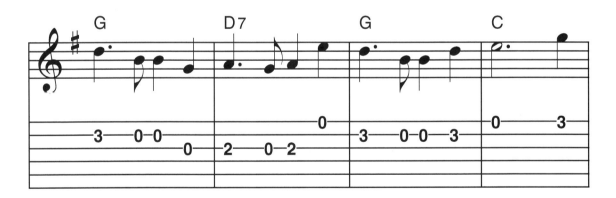

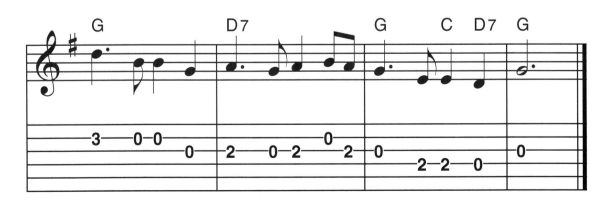

The Foggy, Foggy Dew

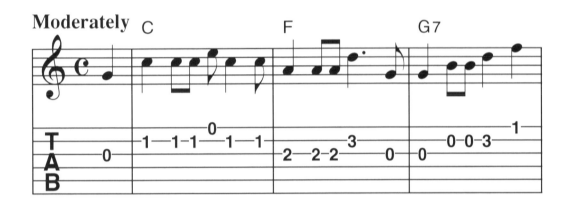

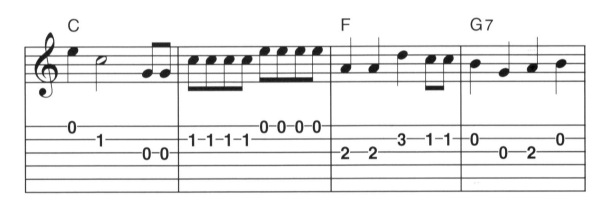

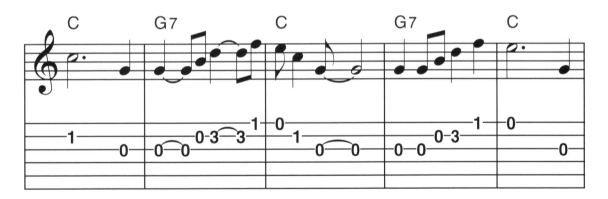

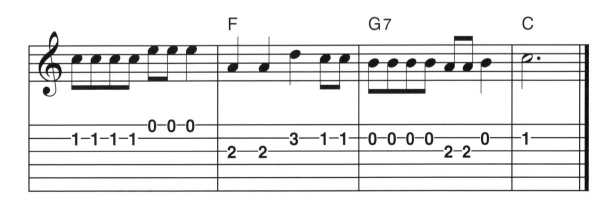

50

Ol' Dan Tucker

Bright Tempo

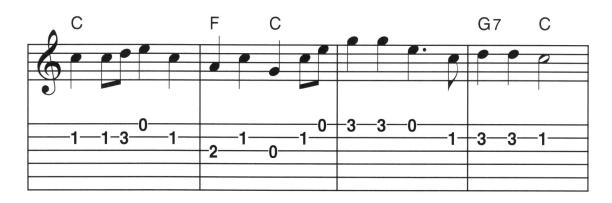

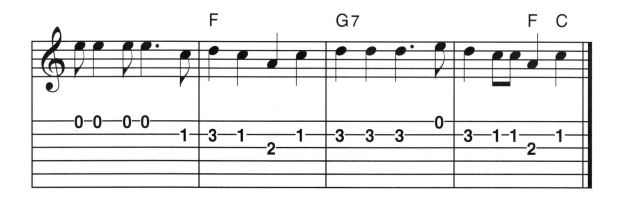

We Shall Meet Some Day

Liza Jane

Lively Tempo

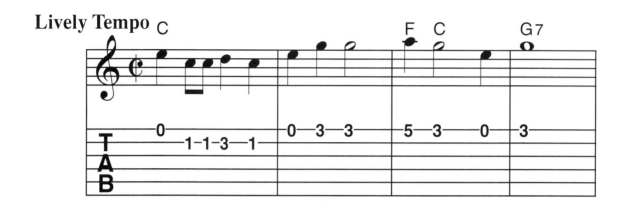

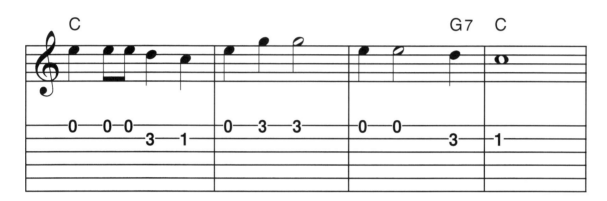

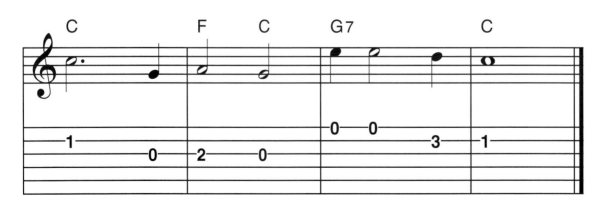

I Never Will Marry

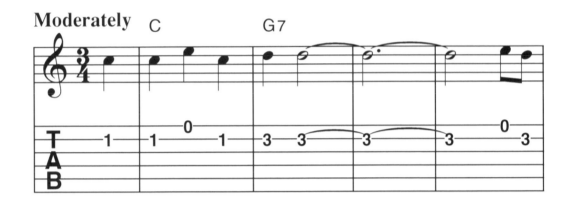

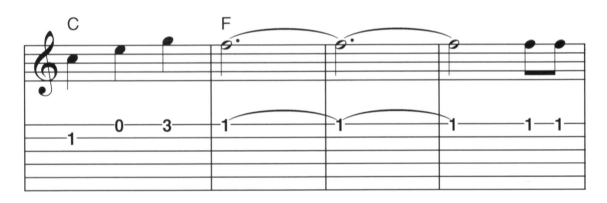

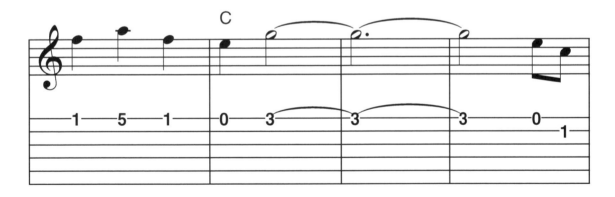

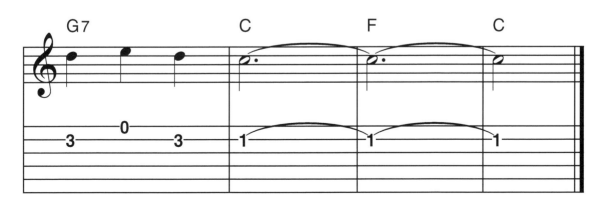

54

Golden Slippers

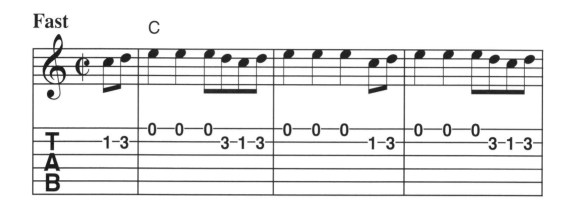

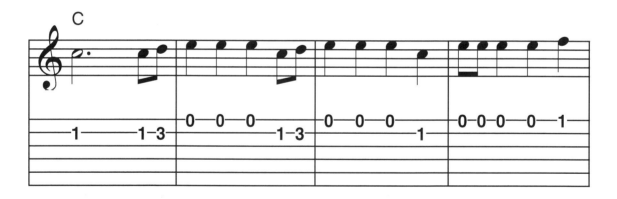

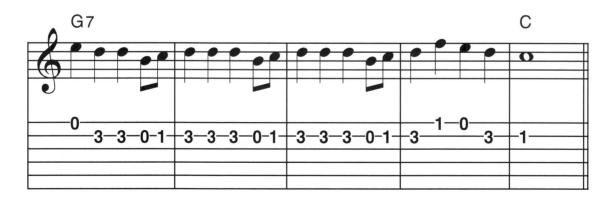

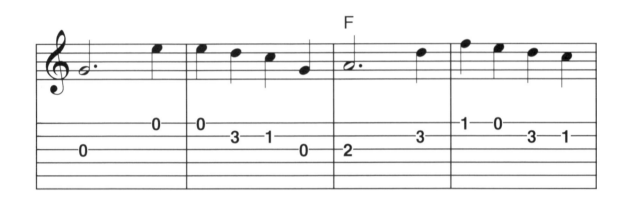

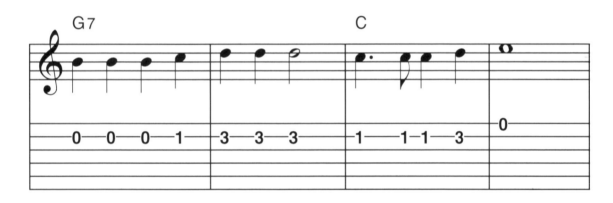

Angel Band

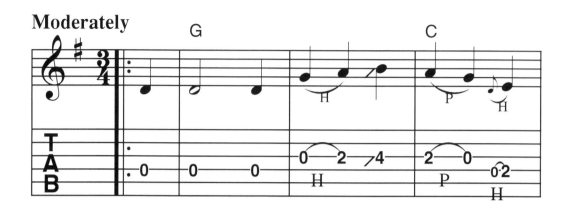

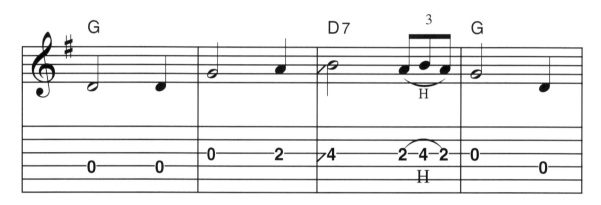

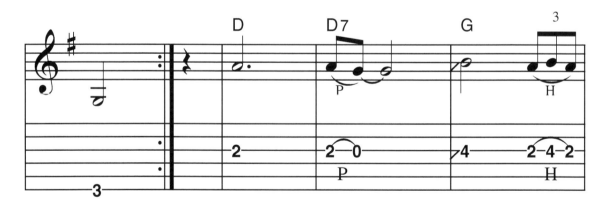

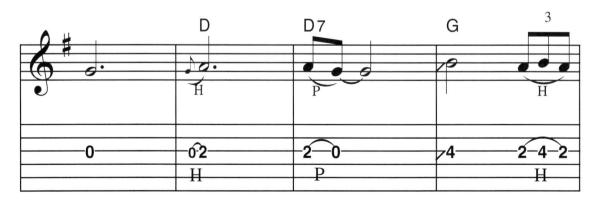

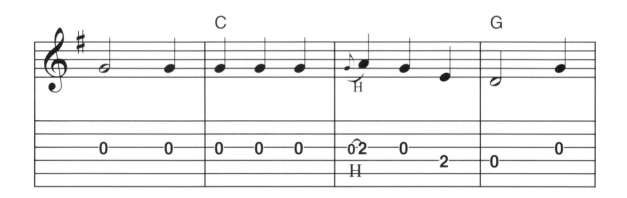

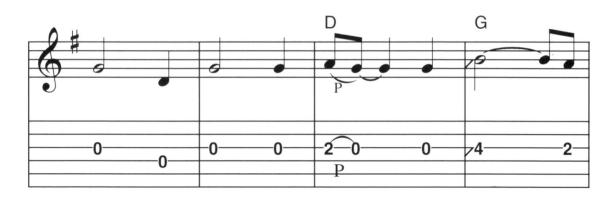

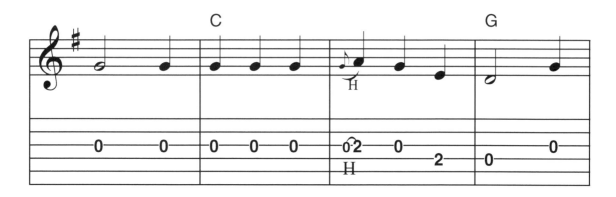

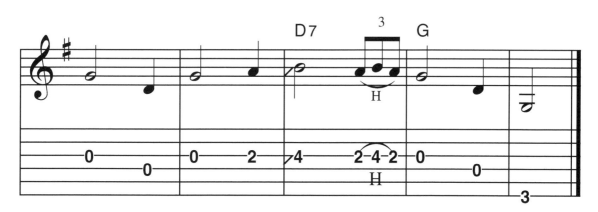

58 Wait Till the Sun Shines, Nellie

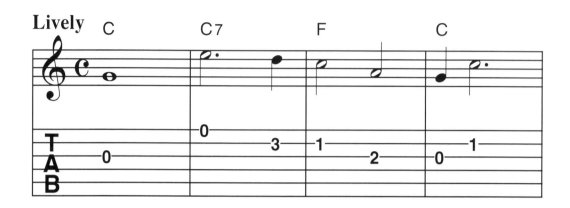

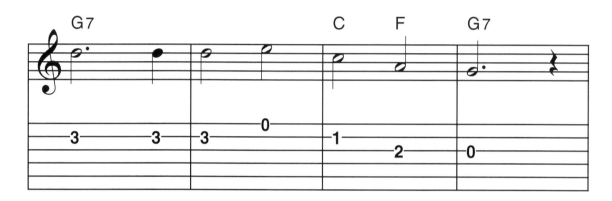

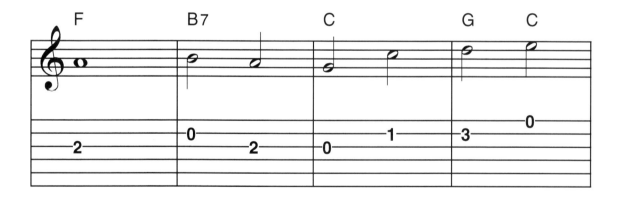

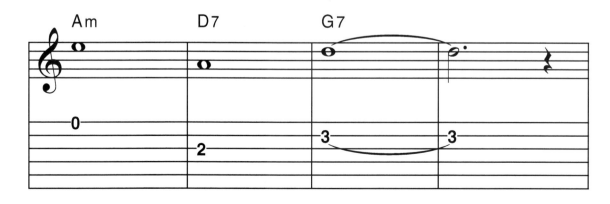

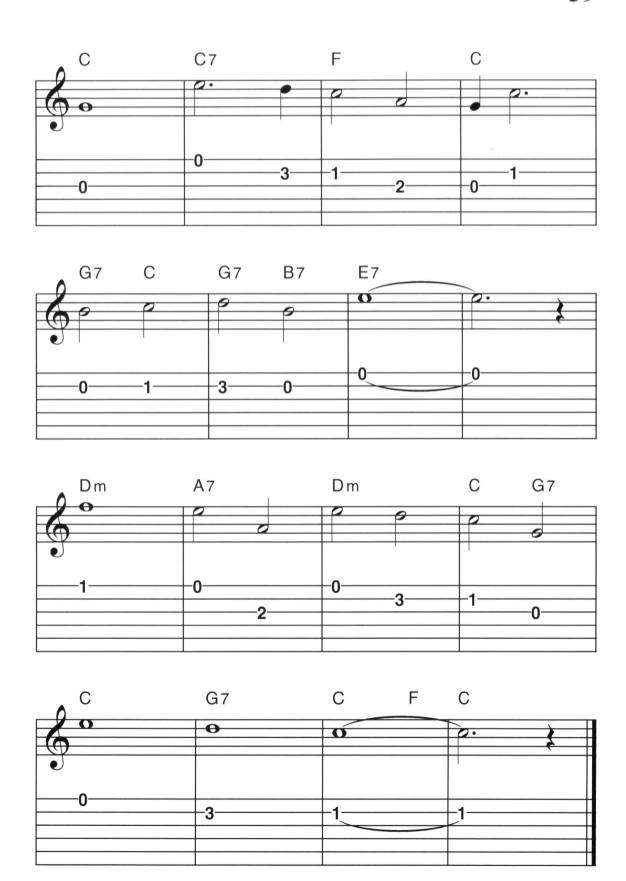

Oh, Sinner Man

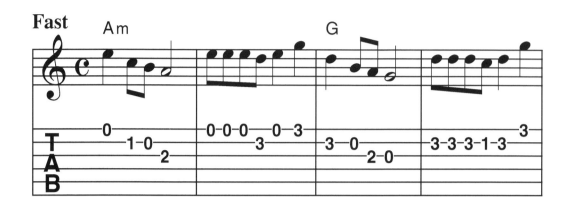

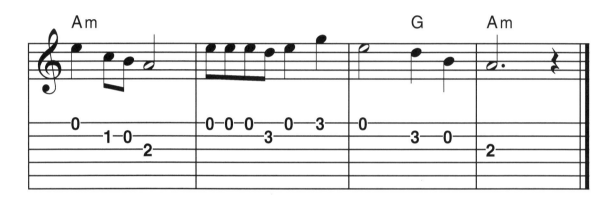

Turkey in the Straw

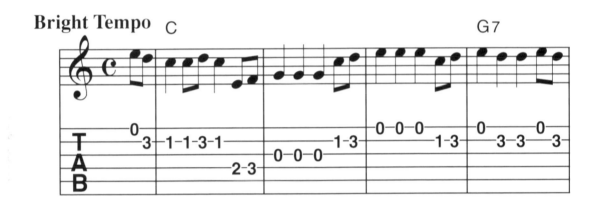

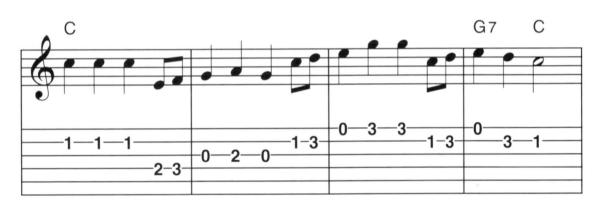

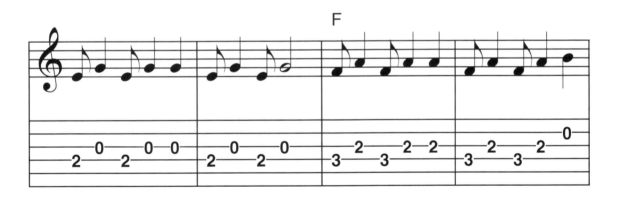

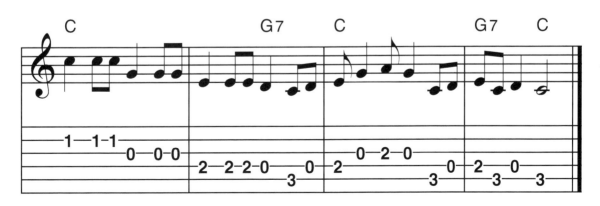

62 Where the Soul Never Dies

Bright Tempo

I Saw Three Ships

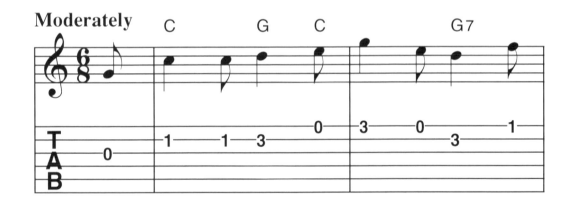

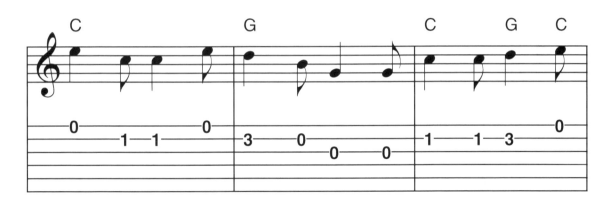

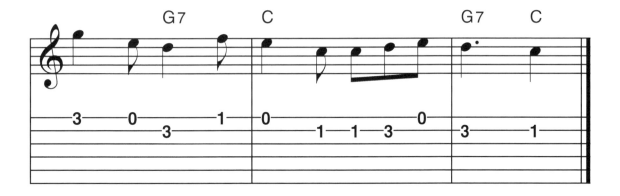

64

Lily of the Valley

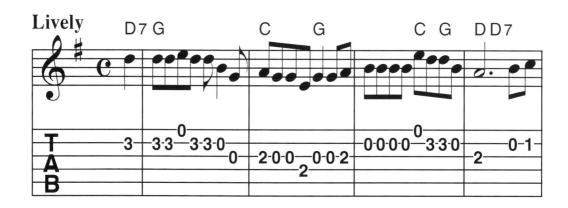

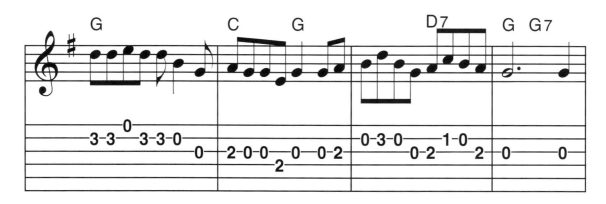

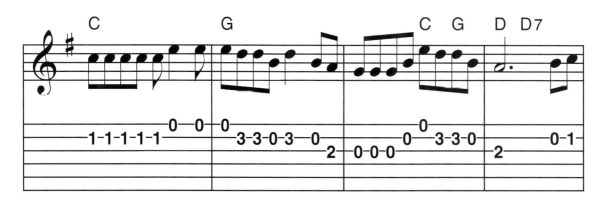

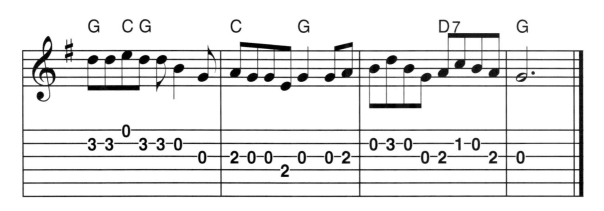

Sail Away, Ladies

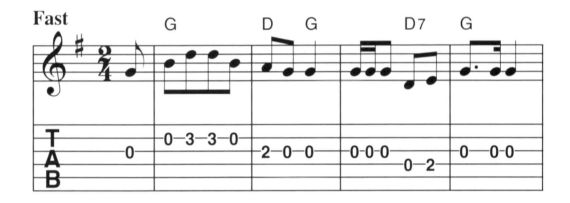

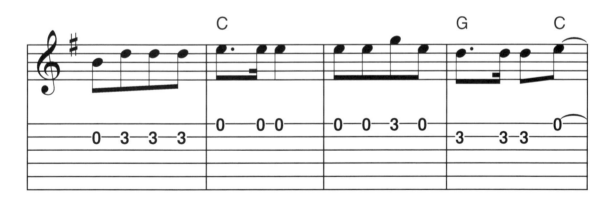

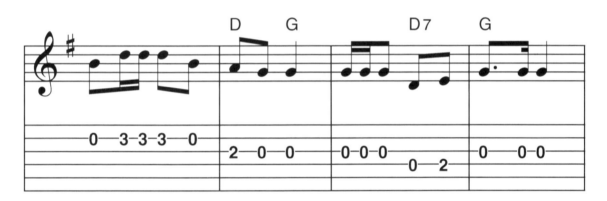

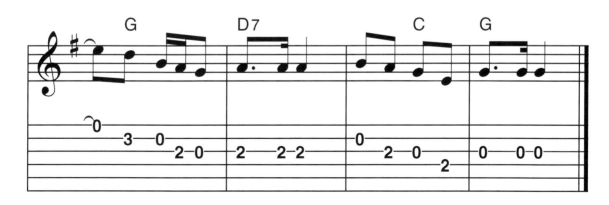

In the Pines

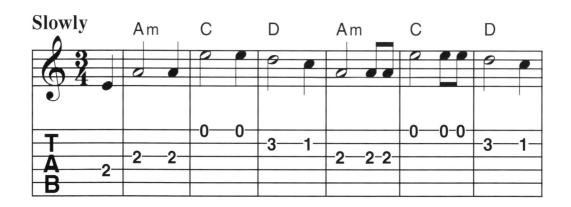

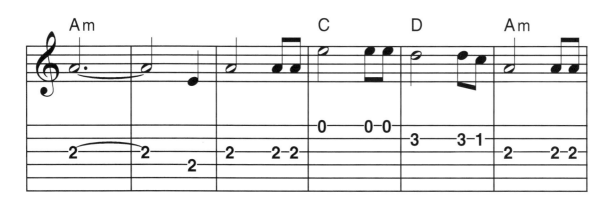

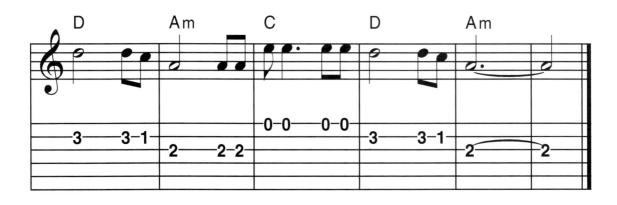

Haul Away Joe

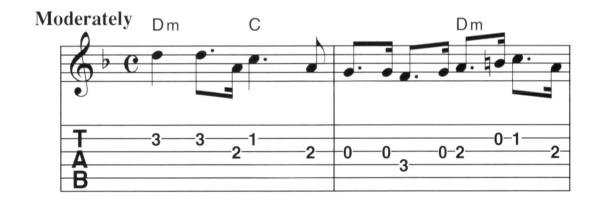

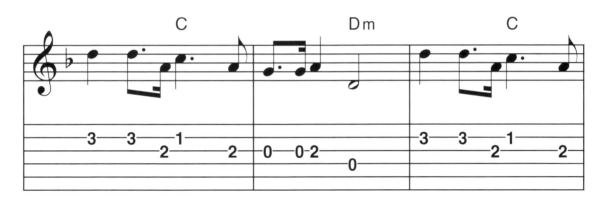

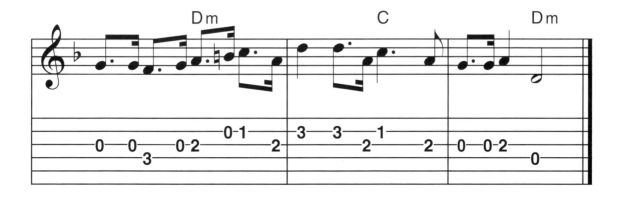

68 The Ship that Never Returned

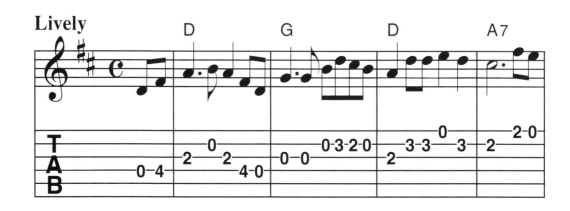

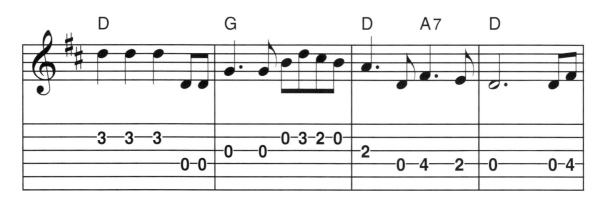

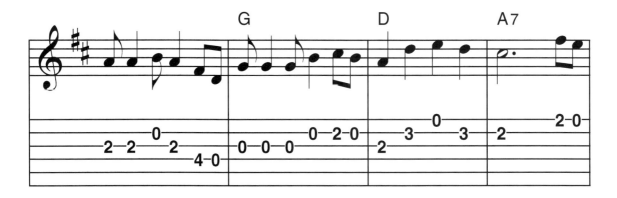

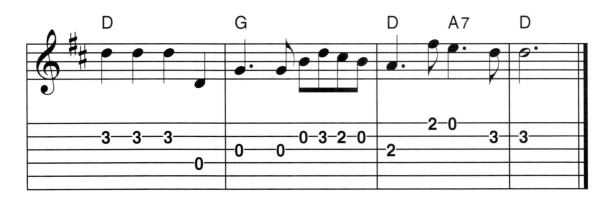

Scarborough Fair

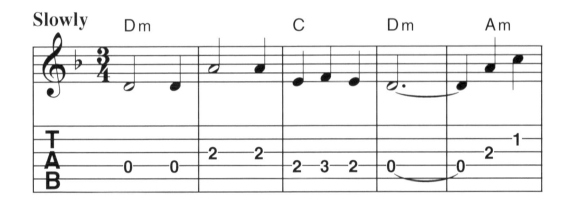

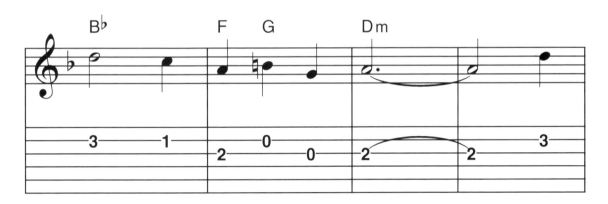

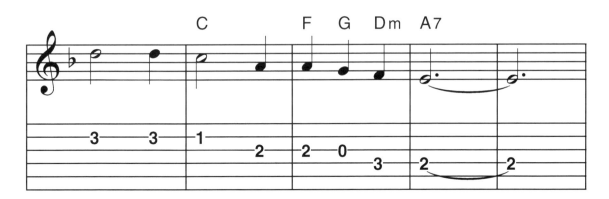

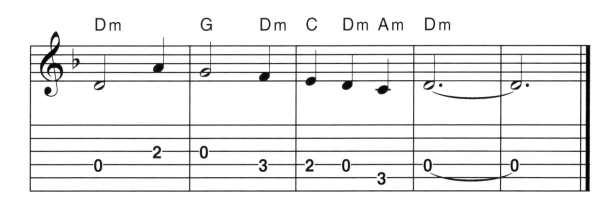

⁷⁰ Life's Railway to Heaven

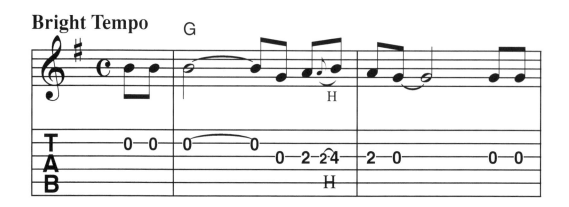

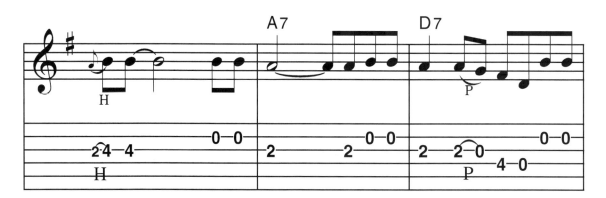

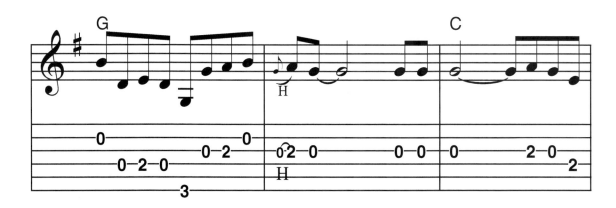

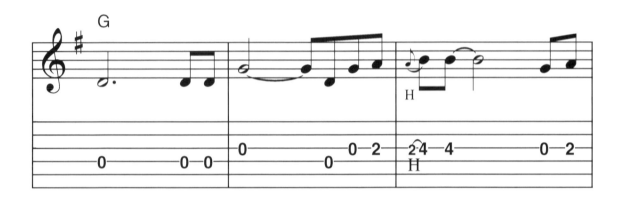

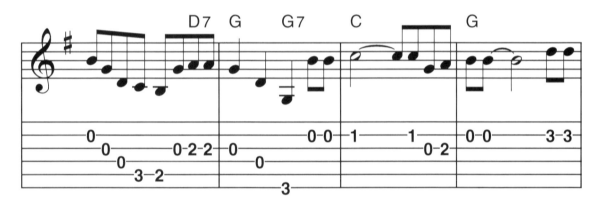

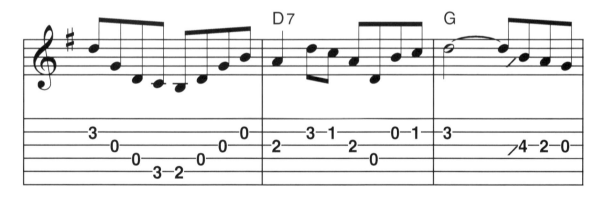

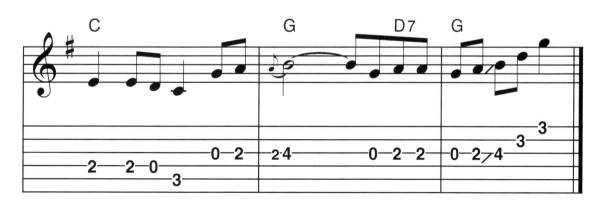

72 # Blow Ye Winds

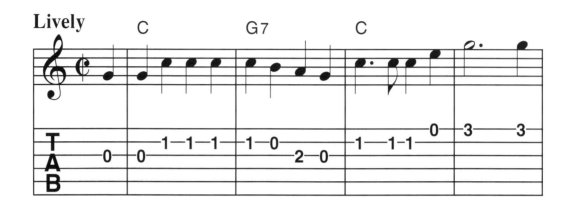

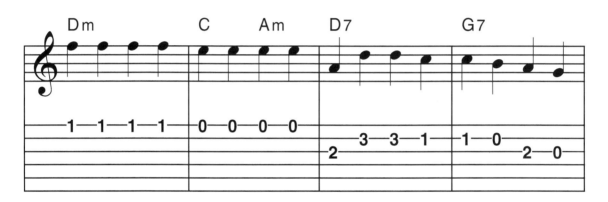

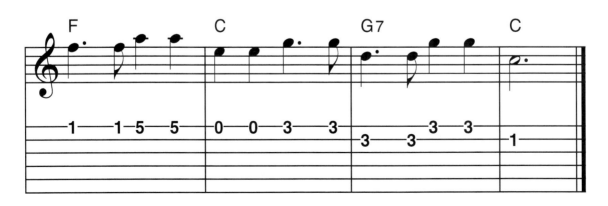

The Roving Gambler

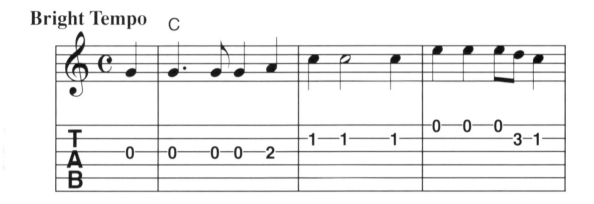

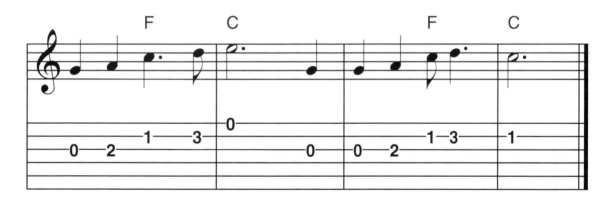

Leaning on the Everlasting Arms

Cripple Creek

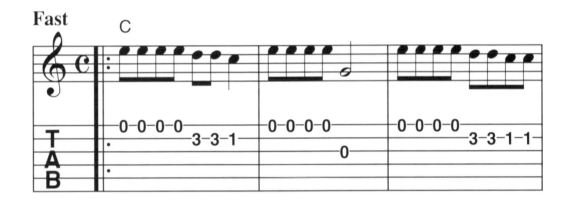

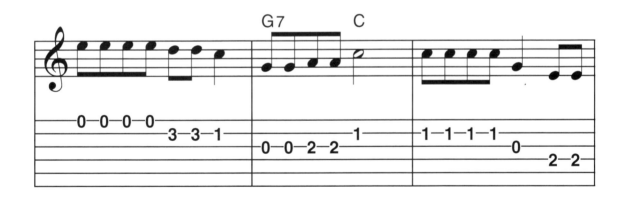

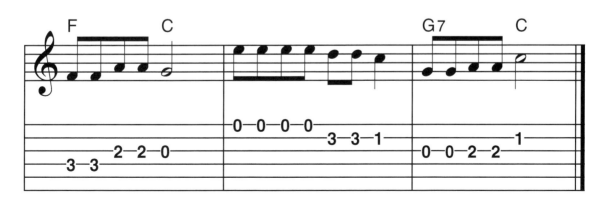

76

I Ride an Old Paint

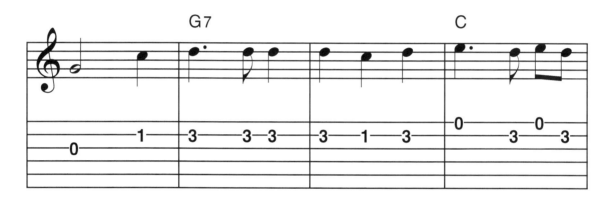

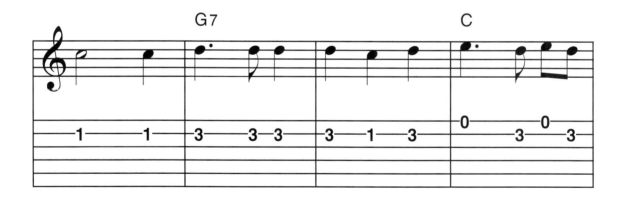

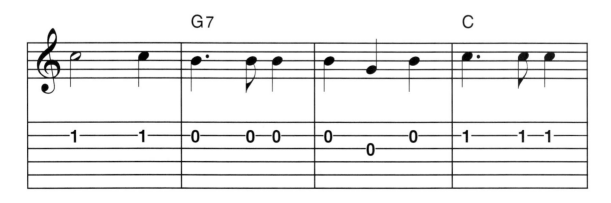

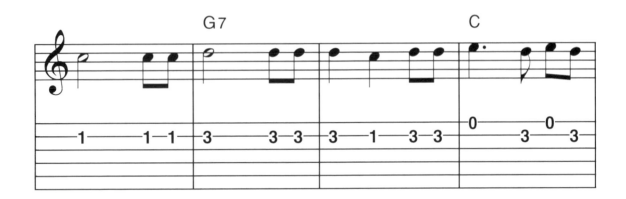

78 It is Well with My Soul

Slowly

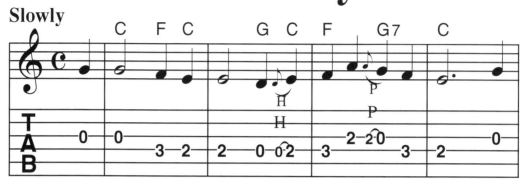

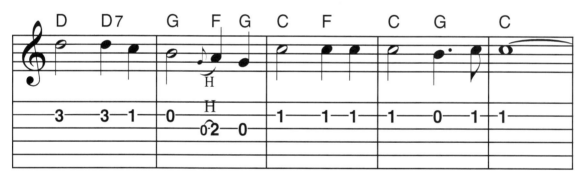

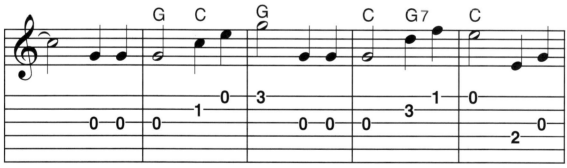

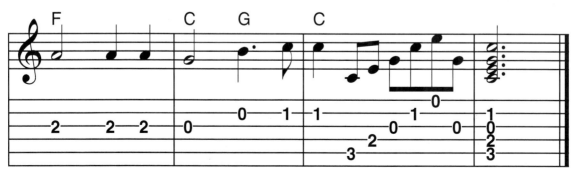

The Chisholm Trail

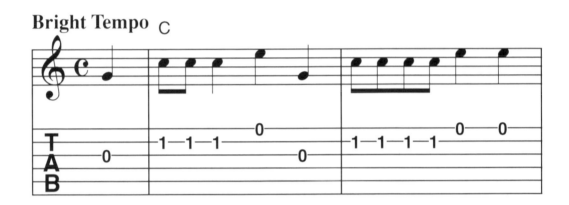

80 My Gal on the Rio Grand

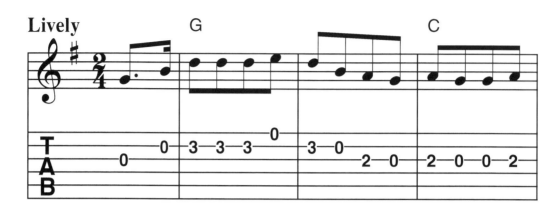

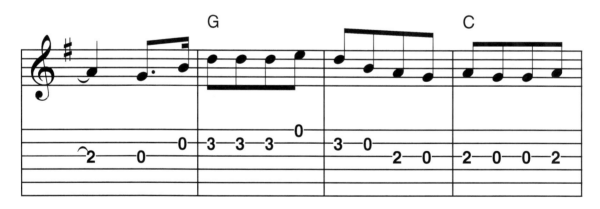

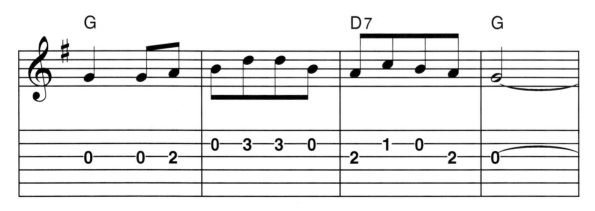

82 House of the Rising Sun

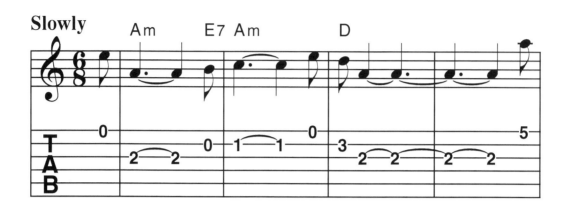

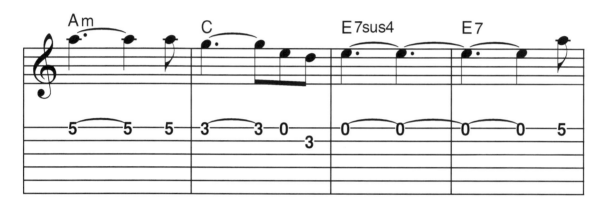

Were You There?

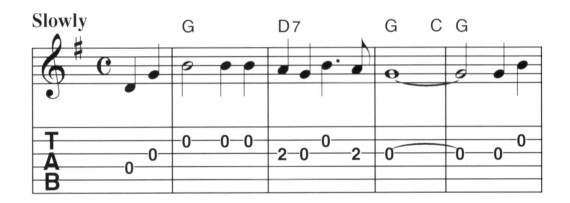

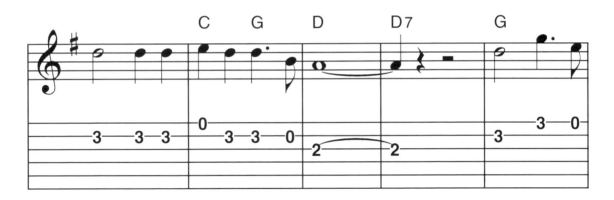

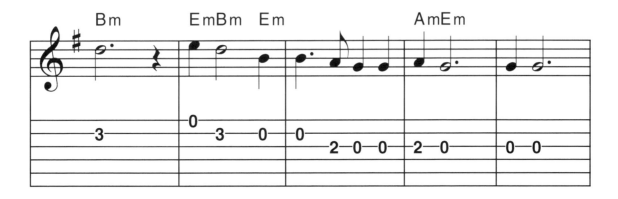

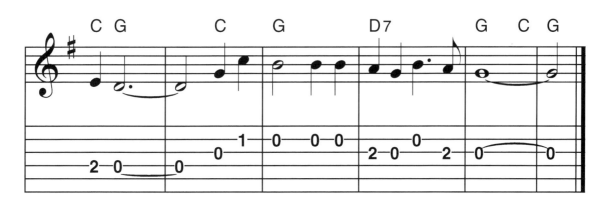

84 **Blackberry Blossom**

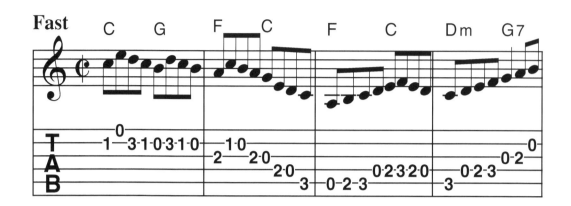

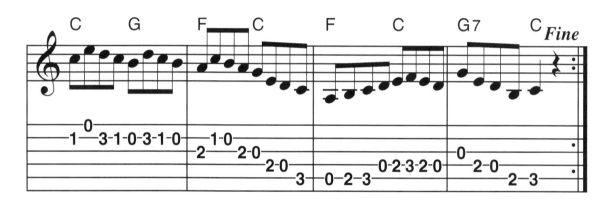

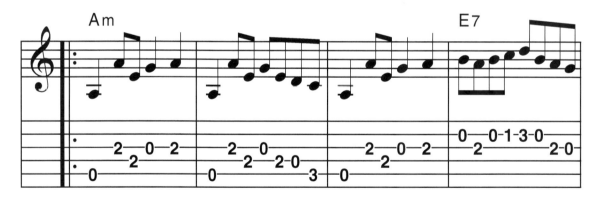

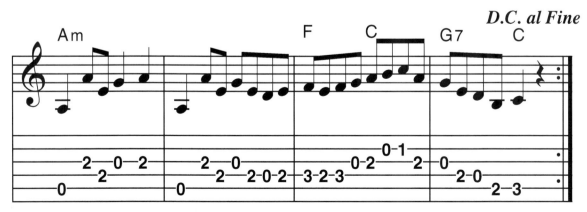

Irish Washerwoman

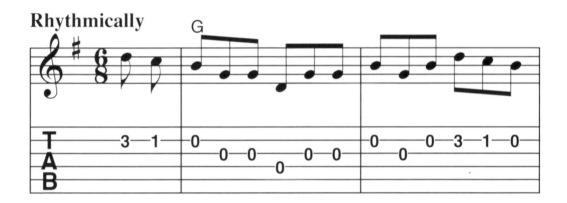

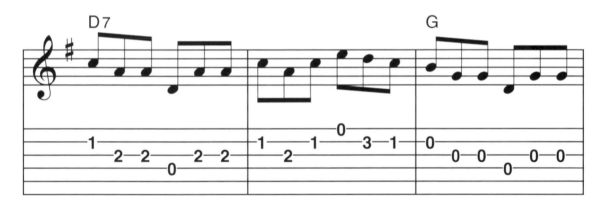

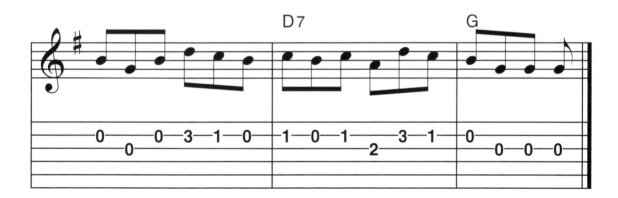

86 Just Over in the Gloryland

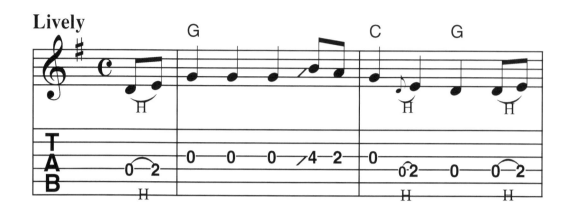

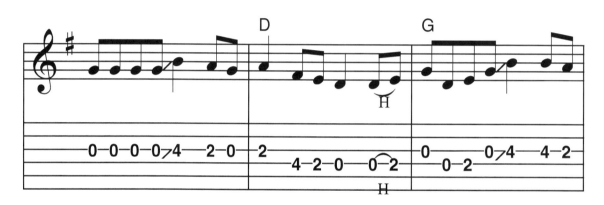

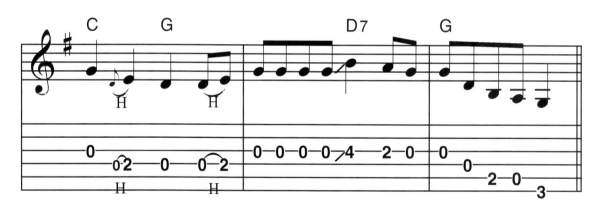

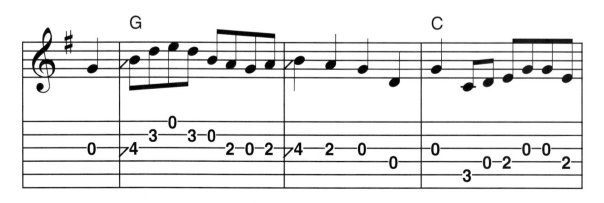

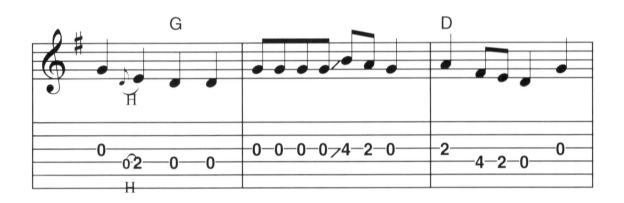

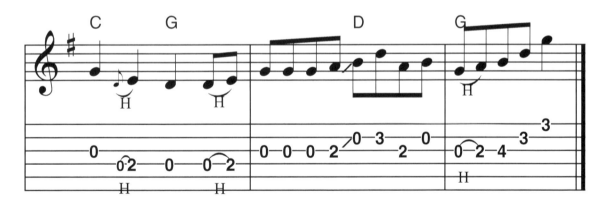

Morrison's Jig

Simple Gifts

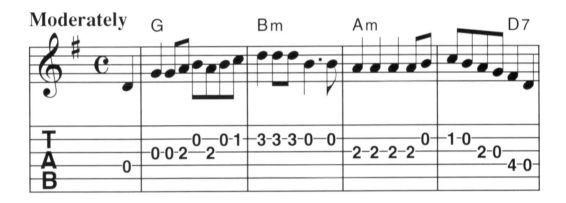

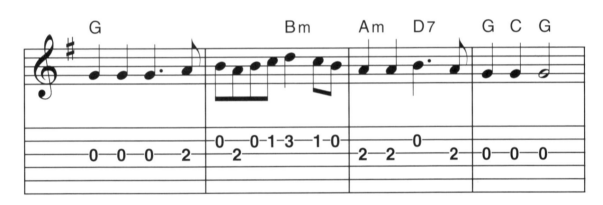

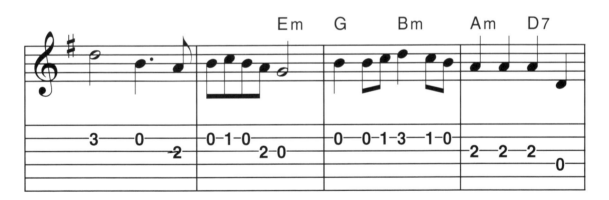

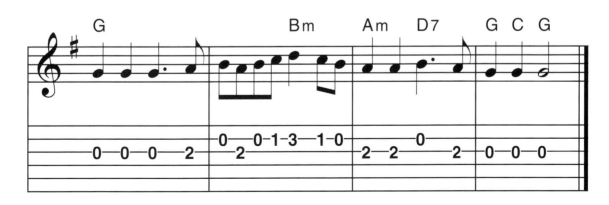

90

Great God, When I Approach Thy Throne

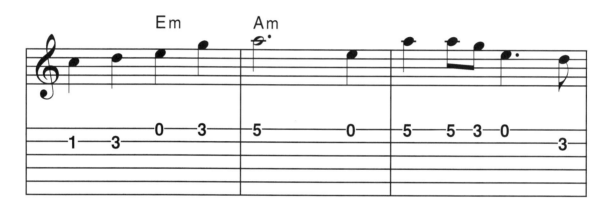

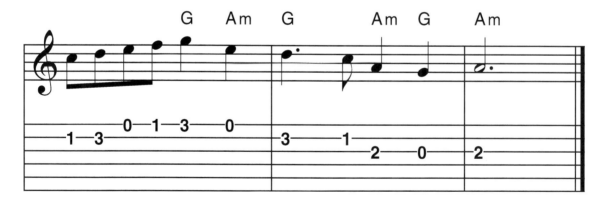

Morning Song

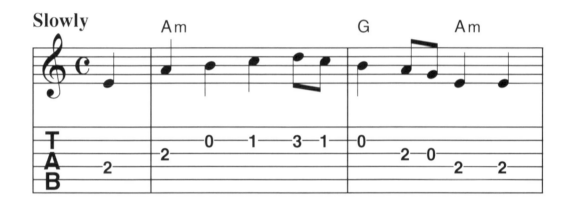

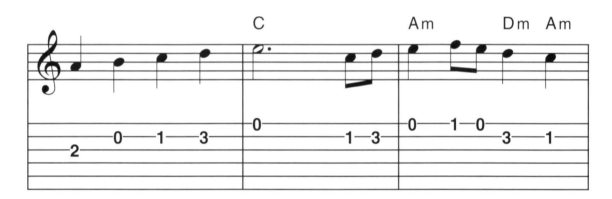

Believe Me if All Those Endearing Young Charms

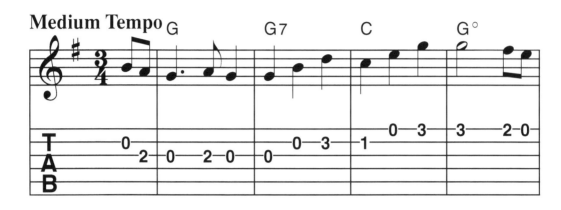

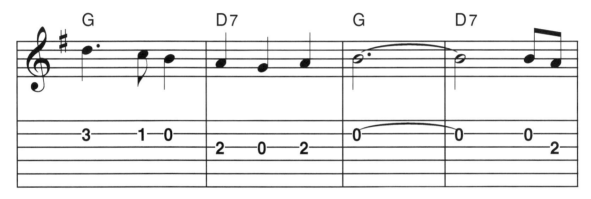

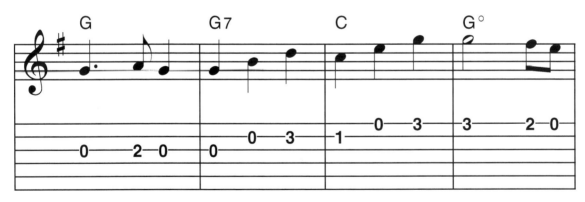

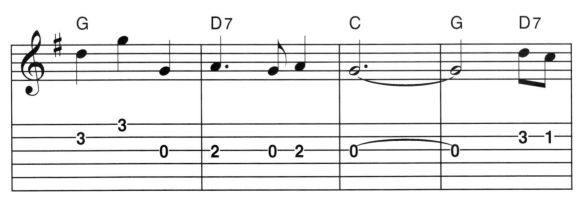

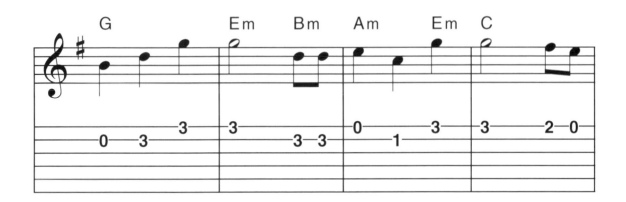

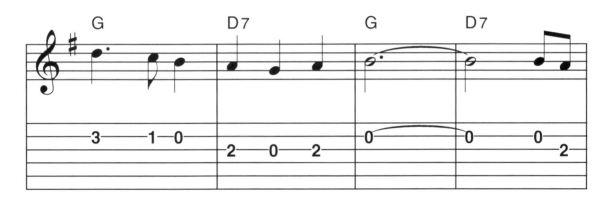

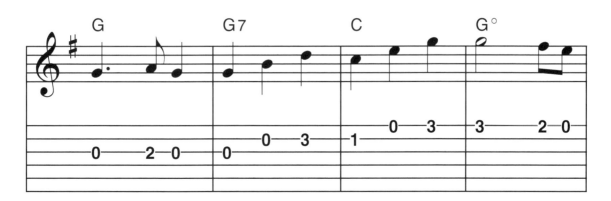

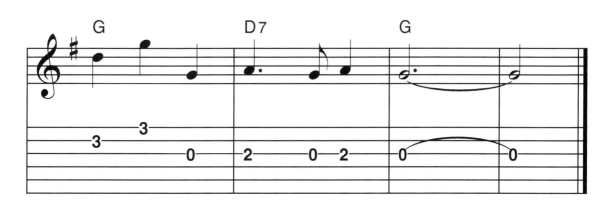

I Love to Tell the Story

Moderately

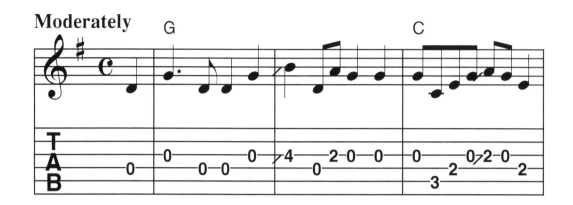

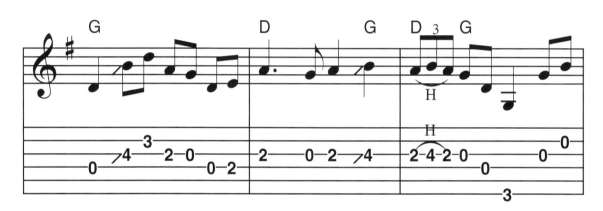

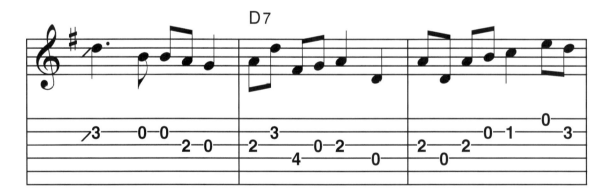

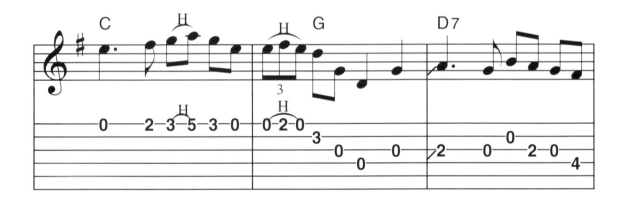

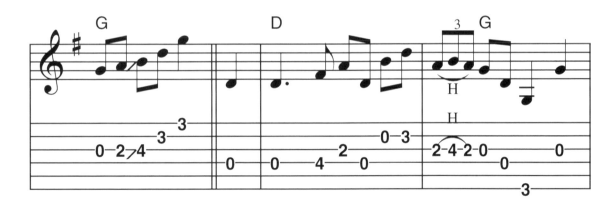

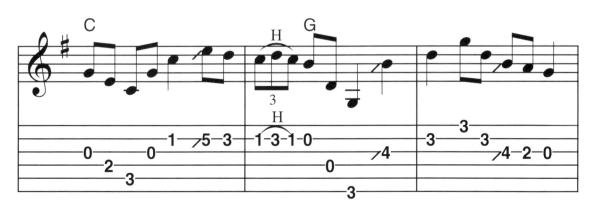

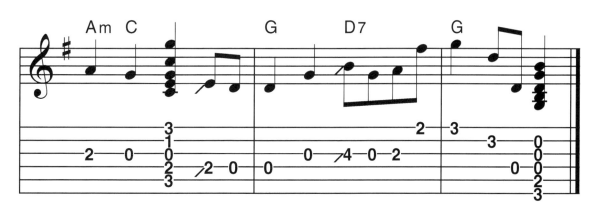

Red Fox Waltz

Medium Tempo

8714430R0

Made in the USA
Charleston, SC
08 July 2011